The Mystery of Seeds

DUANE SHERIFF

The Mystery of Seeds

DISCOVERING THE PROFOUND TRUTHS OF SOWING & REAPING

DUANE SHERIFF

COPYRIGHT

All rights reserved. No portion of this book may be reproduced, stored in a retrieval system, or transmitted in any form or by any means (electronic, mechanical, photocopy, recording, scanning, etc.) without prior written consent of the publisher.

All emphasis within scripture quotations is the author's own.

Unless noted otherwise, all Scripture quotations are from *The New King James Version*. Copyright 1982 by Thomas Nelson. Used by permission. All rights reserved.

The *King James Edition* of the Bible (KJV). 1987 Public Domain in the United States of America.

Scripture quotations marked (TPT) are from *The Passion Translation*®. Copyright © 2017, 2018, 2020 by Passion & Fire Ministries, Inc. Used by permission. All rights reserved. ThePassionTranslation.com.

The *New Living Translation* (NLT) The Holy Bible, New Living Translation, copyright 1996, 2004, 2007 by Tyndale House Foundation. Used by permission of Tyndale House Publishers, Inc., Carol Stream, Illinois 60188. All rights reserved.

The *Amplified Bible, Classic Edition* (AMPC) Copyright 1954, 1958, 1962, 1964, 1965, 1987 by The Lockman Foundation Used by permission. www.Lockman.org

ISBN: 9798998612459
Printed in the United States of America
© 2025 by Victory Life Church
PO Box 427
Durant, OK 74702

dsm@pastorduane.com
580.634.5665

Contents

Chapter 1 | Hidden Mysteries 1

Chapter 2 | The Seed 13

Chapter 3 | The Ground 31

Chapter 4 | Faith as a Seed 39

Chapter 5 | Faith Speaks 51

Chapter 6 | Our Promise Land 62

Chapter 7 | Parable of the Sower 74

Chapter 8 | Reaping Where We Do Not Sow 89

Chapter 1

Hidden Mysteries

You've been given the intimate experience of insight into the hidden mysteries of the realm of heaven's kingdom, but they have not.

Matthew 13:11 (TPT)

The Kingdom of God is a kingdom of paradoxes. On the one hand, it is as simple as a seed. Plant it in good soil, tend and protect it, and eventually that seed will produce a harvest. There's no exceptional skill or formal education required. On the other hand, there are deep profound mysteries hidden in God to be unearthed. When a farmer sows a seed, he does so trusting that seed to produce after its own kind. Whether he sleeps or rises, the seed sprouts and grows. The farmer doesn't have to know how the seed works, but he still benefits from the mystery of the seed (Mark 4:27). The Kingdom of God is like that. Though simple to participate in, it is full of mystery—divine secrets hidden in God. However, these mysteries are not hidden from us, they are hidden for us. Like a seed planted in soil, the mysteries of the Kingdom are hidden and protected from the world. They are reserved for the family of God.

The Holy Spirit unveils each mystery of the Kingdom to us as we walk with God. This keeps us praying, seeking, and knocking at the doors to God's promises and Kingdom realities. It makes our relationship with Jesus an adventure! The mysteries of the Kingdom create within us a hunger for all God has. And as each one is revealed, it proves, yet again, the faithfulness of our God. One mystery gets resolved giving way to a new one to be unveiled. One answered question leads to us asking five more. In this way, the Holy Spirit keeps directing our hearts more deeply into relationship with God.

Humans are wired to seek out answers in the face of mystery and complexity. Is there anyone who doesn't enjoy watching Sherlock Holmes and Professor Watson unravel a mystery? The searching for clues and connecting the dots?. The revelation of "who done it?" and the surprise resolution at the end is an awesome journey to enjoy. The adventure of thinking the culprit was a certain person, and then the surprising discovery of the truth keeps us all connected to the story. Maturing in our walk with God has similar twists and turns at times. How many times have we thought things were one way in the Kingdom only to discover it was quite the opposite? Connecting the dots is what good ministers do in unveiling the progressive mysteries of the Kingdom.

Fear of God

Jesus made it very clear that these mysteries were not for everyone. On the surface, this may seem unfair or unequitable. But when we understand who He shares the mysteries with, we understand why they are hidden from others. Psalm 25:14 says, *"The secret of the Lord is with those who fear Him, and He will show them*

His covenant." Notice that fearing God is how we position our hearts to receive God's secrets—the "mysteries" of His covenant. Fearing God is, in essence, a key to the Kingdom and unveiling of these mysteries (Matt. 16:19). But what does it mean to fear God?

A discussion of the fear of the Lord could be a book of its own, as there is much confusion in the Body of Christ on this topic; hopefully, I can bring clarity through simplicity to that discussion here. First, "the fear of the Lord" is not a demonic or tormenting fear. It doesn't mean to be afraid of God. The fear of the Lord is actually a respect, honor, and reverence toward God. Jesus operated in this kind of "fear" throughout His earthly life and ministry. Isaiah prophesied, *"The Spirit of the LORD shall rest upon Him, The Spirit of wisdom and understanding, The Spirit of counsel and might, The Spirit of knowledge and of the* **fear of the LORD**" (Is. 11:2). Jesus didn't view God with trepidation or a demonic, tormenting fear. Rather He honored God as His Father in worship and respect. If we don't understand there are two types of fear in scripture we will misunderstand the fear of the Lord.

When Jesus was tempted by Satan in the wilderness to worship him as god of this world, Jesus said, *"Away with you Satan! For it is written, 'You shall* **worship** *the Lord your God, and Him only you shall serve.'"* (Matt. 4:10). Jesus was quoting from Deuteronomy 6:13 that says, *"You shall* **fear** *the Lord your God and serve Him."* Notice how Jesus used the words "fear" and "worship" interchangeably. To fear God is to worship Him. It is the beginning of wisdom (Prov. 9:10/Job 28:28). So, it is in the worshipping of God, reverencing and glorifying Him as God that His secrets (mysteries) are revealed.

Jesus also described the results of not fearing God. In Matthew 13:14-15, He quotes Isaiah 6:9-10, saying:

*And in them the prophesy of Isaiah is fulfilled, which says: "Hearing you will hear and shall **not understand**, and seeing you will see and **not perceive**; for the hearts of this people have grown dull. Their ears are hard of hearing, and **their eyes they have closed**, lest they should see with their eyes and hear with their ears, lest they should understand with their hearts and turn, so that I should heal them."*

Notice that God did not close His eyes, but they closed theirs. They chose not to hear or see. Isaiah also brings out this poor choice on their part—*"Who has believed our report? And to whom has the arm of the Lord been revealed?"* (Is. 53:1). Some believed it but many did not. Some had a sensitive and receiving heart, while others had a hard heart that led to unbelief. If we dive deeper into the prophecy Jesus was quoting from Isaiah, we read:

> *Therefore the Lord said: "Inasmuch as these people draw near with their mouths and honor Me with their lips, but have removed their hearts far from me, and **their fear** toward Me is taught by the commandment of men [...] for the wisdom of their wise men shall perish, and the understanding of their prudent men shall be hidden."*

Isaiah 29:13-14

At the time of Isaiah's writing (and Jesus' ministry) many of the Jewish people did not have a heart-felt fear or reverence of God, but rather a fear taught to them by man. Over time, they allowed their hearts to become dull of hearing and hardened to His leading. This deafened and blinded them to the mysteries of the Kingdom and kept them from repentance. God delights in revealing the secrets of His covenant to those who fear Him (Psalm 25:14). The mysteries of the Kingdom were hidden from many of the Jews because of their own choice to not fear or worship God from their hearts. May that never be said of us.

Believing Jews

The early church was comprised of believing Jews. On the day of Pentecost it was 120 Jews in the upper room. The 3000 saved in one day on the day of Pentecost, were Jews (Acts 2:41). Then Acts 4:4 records another 5000 becoming believers. Mary and Joseph were Jews, John the Baptist was a Jew, and the apostles were all Jews that received salvation and their eyes were opened because they feared God. The prophets that brought us the revelation of who Jesus is and how He would save us were Jews. Their eyes were opened and they had understanding (wisdom) because they all feared God. Others chose to close their eyes and ears missing the mystery of God made flesh among them.

Stewards

As believers, we've been made stewards of the mysteries of God (1 Cor. 4:1). And as stewards, Paul says, *"it is required [...] that one be found faithful"* (vs. 2). The Holy Spirit reveals the divine, life-changing secrets of the Kingdom to faithful men and women who will honor God from their hearts, applying each mystery as it is revealed (and in the case of teachers, sharing them in accuracy, simplicity, and confidence).

Paul revealed one of the chief mysteries of the Kingdom in 1 Timothy. He called it the "mystery of godliness." Remember, we are stewards of this mystery. Paul teaches:

> *And without controversy great is the **mystery of godliness**: God was manifest in the flesh, justified in the Spirit, seen by angels, preached among the Gentiles, believed on in the world, received up in glory.*
>
> 1 Timothy 3:16

WOW! This one verse embodies the mystery of our great salvation and godliness. In Christ, God became one of us. He became Immanuel, God with us (Matt. 1:23). He was seen in the entire angelic world when He died for our sins and was raised from the dead. He stripped Satan and every demonic host of the authority Adam relinquished through sin and set the precedent for proclaiming His gospel to every tribe and tongue on the planet (Col. 2:15). Those who believed—both Jew and Gentile—received salvation because Jesus returned to glory and was seated at the right hand of the throne of God. Of that mystery, Paul asked, *"that utterance may be given to me, that I may open my mouth boldly to make known the* **mystery of the gospel***"* (Eph. 6:19).

There are so many wonderful mysteries to be unearthed and shared from the Holy Scriptures: the mystery of Christ in us, the hope of glory (Col. 1:27); the mysteries of the Kingdom (Mark 4:11); the mystery of His will according to His good pleasure which He purposed in Himself (Eph. 1:9—that's a good one); the mystery of iniquity (2 Thess. 2:7 KJV); the mystery of Israel's blindness (Rom. 11:25); the mystery of the resurrection of our bodies (1 Cor. 15:51-54); the mystery of God's wisdom hidden from Satan at the cross; and many more. Take a look at this profound mystery:

> *But we speak the wisdom of God in a* **mystery***, the hidden wisdom which God ordained before the ages for our glory, which none of the rulers of this age knew; for* **had they known***, they would not have crucified the Lord of glory.*
>
> 1 Corinthians 2:7-8

That is an over-the-top statement! The "rulers of this age" refer to Satan and the wicked spiritual hosts of this world. Had they known how we would be reconciled to God and made the very body of Christ in the earth, with Jesus as the head, they would never have crucified Jesus. But God hid this wisdom from them for our benefit!

In John 12:24 Jesus says, *"Most assuredly, I say to you, unless a grain of wheat falls into the ground and dies, it remains alone; but if it dies, it produces much grain."* This verse is a direct reference to the mystery of Jesus' death as a seed. Had Jesus not gone to the cross and willfully taken our sins upon Himself, He would still be here in bodily form alone. He would have never died. (Sin brings death, and Jesus had no sin.) But had He remained, He would have remained alone. There would have been no harvest from His life given. We are the harvest of that seed sown, Christ's sacrifice. This is what Jesus meant when He told the disciples it was better that He go away and the Holy Spirit come (John 16:7). Jesus had faith in the seed of His life. Now we, as born-again believers, and carriers of His Spirit, are a worldwide expression of God's power and love. Jesus, in a physical body, was restricted to one geographic location. We, as members of His body, are not. We are the "much grain" or fruit of His seed—the precious seed of His life. Now His body is not one member, but many (1 Cor. 12:12).

Each mystery of the Kingdom is thus hidden—not *from* us, but *for* us—in seed form. Seeds are some of life's greatest blessings, both physically and spiritually. They are vehicles of growth, provision, and transformation in tiny, portable packages and they are one of the primary ways God works in our lives. The fourth chapter of Mark reveals the power and potential of God's Word as seed working in the human heart. And though we'll review that chapter in depth in another portion of this book, allow me to lay a foundational truth of God's immutable law of seeds.

Law Of Seeds

> *While the earth remains,* **seedtime and harvest,** *cold and heat, winter and summer, and day and night shall not cease.*
>
> Genesis 8:22

Seedtime and harvest are changeless and reliable laws of creation. As long as the earth remains, Genesis says, these things will be constants. What we sow, we will reap. As sure as the sun rises and sets each day, the Earth will experience seasons of cold and heat, winter and summer. We can trust these certainties in an uncertain world. We can use them to order our lives. Our entire world rotates around these God-ordained natural laws, and God uses these familiar cycles around us to reveal and explain the mystery of His Kingdom.

Just like these laws of nature allow us to configure our lives to receive God's blessing of provision, the Kingdom of God also contains laws (or principles) that work for our benefit. Seedtime and harvest is one of those laws. And like all laws, it is non-discriminatory. It works for or against us all without prejudice, bias, or partiality. If we plant the seed of God's Word in our heart—let's say His promise of peace—and watch over that seed, protecting and watering that seed, it will grow and produce the fruit of peace in our lives—regardless of the circumstances we face (Is. 26:3). If, however, we choose not to plant that seed, or we neglect the seed after it is planted, we won't experience its fruit.

Anything we need in this life can be found in seed form in the Word of God. We just have to understand and apply it properly in our lives. This law allows for the provision and blessing of God to be distributed to everyone without bias. We can sow to the kind of life we desire to have and experience.

Isaiah 55:10 says that God gives seed to the Sower and bread to the eater. Isaiah continues, **"So shall My word be** *that goes forth from My mouth; it shall not return to Me void, but it shall accomplish what I please, and it shall prosper in the thing for which I sent it"* (vs. 11). God's Word is seed. And just like physical seed must be sown into the ground to produce bread (or, more accurately, the wheat we use to make bread), so God's Word must be sown in our hearts where it will produce fruit in our lives to glorify God. As believers who desire to participate in all the blessings of God, we have to learn to sow God's Word as a seed. Only then will we develop into mature believers and be able to reap His promises.

There is a seed—a promise—for every need in our lives. For years, I labored under the misconception that God was a respecter of persons. I believed He favored some over others, and I was an "other." (Sometimes, I felt like an "other" to the "others.") But scripture says that God makes the sun to rise on the evil and the good; He sends rain to the just and unjust (Matt. 5:45). God has established this principle of seedtime and harvest as an eternal law. It will work for anyone who chooses to mix faith with His Word (Heb. 4:2).

The spiritual laws of God's Kingdom are as reliable and constant as the laws of nature. Romans chapter one says that God has revealed Himself, even His eternal power and Godhead, through creation (Rom. 1:20). Some people have perverted that truth. They say that creation *is* God. And while God can certainly reveal Himself through a tree or sunrise, the tree or sun is not God. The weather is not God. The stars in the sky are not God either. God may reveal Himself in the universe, but those things seen simply unveil His unseen attributes. Scripture teaches, *"The heavens declare the glory of God; and the firmament shows His handiwork"* (Psalm 19:1).

The laws of nature declare God's righteousness (Psalm 50:6). You cannot look at the universe and say there is no God. The perfect order of the planets, the vastness of space, the placement of the stars and galaxies, the earth, sun, and moon all declare God's glory. He reveals Himself throughout creation, for the seen came out of the unseen. They mirror one another. Consider this: There is no earthly life independent of the sun. And there is no eternal life independent of the Son.

Gravity is an eternal, nonbiased law of nature. God built it into the fabric of creation. It is reliable and constant. But it can be violated. If we sovereignly choose to violate the law of gravity and jump off a building, what God intended for our good will become a curse. That's not God's fault. He is not the author of any curse. It is simply a law of nature. Electricity is another such law. It doesn't care who you are or what you look like. If you touch a screwdriver to the metal plate of an electrical outlet, you're going to feel it. I've mishandled electricity a couple of times, and it has not been good. In fact, I'm thankful to be alive. That's why I don't touch electricity anymore. Lightning struck my peanut brain and wisdom kicked in. Now, in my mind, electricity has a sign on it saying, "Duane, do not touch!"

Other laws can override or temporarily suspend natural laws, but the overridden law does not cease to exist. Every time I get on a plane, I'm reminded that cooperating with the laws of aerodynamics can cause a humongous chunk of metal to fly. But that doesn't mean I can fly independent of the laws of aerodynamics. Turn that higher law off in midair and gravity will kick in. Every time I turn on a light or enjoy refrigeration, I thank God that someone learned how to harness electricity (thank you Benjamin Franklin). I may not fully understand these laws, but can enjoy them, nonetheless. Natural law is eternal and nondiscriminatory. It works for everyone. Had people in Biblical times known how to cooperate with these laws, artificial light and airplanes could have been accessed and enjoyed in Jesus' day. That mystery was there but hidden. How many more are still there, even in the natural, and are currently hidden?

In Romans 8:2, Paul talks about the laws that govern our life in Christ. He tells the believers in Rome that the "law of life" supersedes the "law of sin and death" when we walk after the Spirit. And in Romans three, Paul talks about the "law of faith" (vs. 27). He says that Jews with the law and Gentiles outside the law both fall short of God's standard, even when they do what is right in their own eyes. Because of the grace and mercy of God, there is no benefit to boasting. Works, whether works of the law or of the flesh, accomplish nothing of eternal value. God is under no obligation to save any of us. Yet all who believe—both Jew and Gentile—are justified freely by His grace. For we are saved through "the law of faith" (Rom. 3:27-29).

Notice that Paul calls each of these spiritual principals "laws." As we've seen, natural laws are reliable. So, too, are the laws that govern God's Kingdom. In Romans chapter ten, we read that *"faith comes by hearing, and hearing by the Word of God"* (vs. 17). This is a law of faith. So, if you are in need of faith, listen to God's Word. But don't stop there. James 2:20 and 26 say, *"Faith without works [action] is dead."* You have to act on your faith in order for that faith to be productive. You can't believe one way and act another. Neither can you have true biblical faith and not back up those words of faith with action. It is a law.

Hundreds of laws govern God's Kingdom, and God wants us to know each one. That's one of the reasons He gave us His Word. God wants to reveal the mysteries of the Kingdom to us all. Yet Paul declares that *"we see through a glass, darkly"* (1 Cor. 13:12 KJV). We don't know it all. But one day—when Jesus returns or He appears at our death—we will know "face to face." We will know even as we are known (1 Cor. 13:12). Until then, God reveals the mysteries of His Kingdom to us progressively, from glory to glory, as we remain teachable before Him (2 Cor. 3:18). As we fear God with a wholesome fear, expect to have these mysteries revealed. The mysteries that rotate around seeds are profound and revealed to all who fear Him. God, in partnership with us and the law of seeds, allows us to chart the kind of life we desire to live.

Chapter 2
The Seed

So is the kingdom of God, as if a man should cast seed into the ground.

Mark 4:26 (KJV)

Everything in the Kingdom revolves around seeds—from what we receive from God to the way we treat others.

Do not be deceived, God is not mocked; for whatever a man sows, that he will also reap. For he who sows to his flesh will of the flesh reap corruption, but he who sows to the Spirit will of the Spirit reap everlasting life. And let us not grow weary while doing good, for in due season we shall reap if we do not lose heart. Therefore, as we have opportunity, let us do good to all, especially to those who are of the household of faith.

Galatians 6:7-10

Notice the initial admonition in this passage is to not be deceived. God warns us that deception in this area of sowing and reaping is common. I've even heard of ministers declaring sowing and reaping is not a new covenant principle and doesn't apply to new believers. WOW! Many people do not heed scripture's warning here. Some people are deceived into thinking there are no consequences to sowing to the flesh. Others doubt the blessing of sowing to the spirit. But regardless of man's interpretation or reservation, God is not mocked. God's Word is sure. We will reap a harvest off whatever seed we sow.

A good example is the life of Jacob (told in Genesis 25 and 27). He deceived his father Isaac using the skin of a goat. He submitted to his mother's plan to steal his brother Esau's birthright. Though the brothers were twins, Esau was born before Jacob so was considered the first born. Rebekah, Jacob's mother, killed two goats and made a stew for Jacob to take to his father while Esau was out hunting for venison. She dressed Jacob in those goat skins to deceive Isaac into thinking Jacob was really Esau. Esau was a hairy man whereas Jacob had smooth skin. Since Isaac was nearly blind, she felt like this scheme would work; and it did. However, this was a bad seed sown in Jacob's life. Not only did Jacob have to leave home to keep his brother from killing him, but years also later his own sons deceived him with the blood of a goat. Jacob's sons had sold their brother Joseph into slavery and used the blood of a goat to cover his cloak with blood to convince their father he had been killed by a wild animal (Gen. 37). Remember, brothers and sisters, that every seed we sow yields a harvest.

If we sow to our flesh, scripture says we will **of our flesh** *reap corruption*. It is important to notice that corruption does not come from God. We cannot yield to the temptations of our flesh, then blame God for the consequences of our bad choices. God didn't sow the seed. He is not to blame for the harvest. Any corruption we reap in life comes from our flesh, not God. But the scripture also says that if we sow to the spirit, we will **of the spirit** *reap everlasting life*. Jesus *is* the Lord of the Harvest on the good seeds we sow. And He is faithful. If we do not abort the process, we will reap a harvest of good.

Immediately after discussing how the principle of sowing and reaping works, Paul transitions into the way we treat others. But this is not a change of subject. Paul ties these thoughts together with the word "therefore." That's like saying, "because you understand this thing, do this other thing." Or "because you understand sowing and reaping do good to others." That's because the way we treat other people is a seed we sow (Gal. 6:10).

Doing good to others and treating them as we wish to be treated is a good seed. Sleeping with your neighbor's spouse is a bad seed. So is stealing time from your boss. Don't sow those kinds of seeds. Purpose to sow good seeds in every relationship you have and fulfill the law of love from Romans thirteen: *"Love worketh no ill to his neighbor: therefore love is the fulfilling of the law."* (Rom. 13:10, KJV). If you do sow a bad seed, repent quickly. Believe for crop failure on that seed and put good seeds back into the ground of your relationships. Otherwise, your harvest will look like the words of Proverbs 26:27 which says, *"Whoever digs a pit will fall into it, and he who rolls a stone will have it roll back on him."* Even the golden rule, "do unto others as you would have done unto you," has to do with sowing and reaping. Many people—both saved and lost—foolishly overlook this truth (Matt. 7:12). They are ensnared by their own words or actions in the harming of others. Their plots of harm come back to bite them. We see an example of this when reading the story of Esther.

Haman

Haman, the Agagite, hated God's people. When he discovered that a fellow official in Xerxes court was a Jew, he plotted to destroy the man (along with every Jew in Persia). Mordecai (the fellow official) was devoted to God and served the king faithfully. At one time, Mordecai even saved the king's life. But when Mordecai refused to bow before Haman, Haman's hatred grew.

He couldn't wait for his plan against the Jews to unfold. He built gallows, hoping to see Mordecai hanged. When Queen Esther (also a Jew) learned what Haman was attempting to do, she risked her life to reveal his plot. The king allowed the Jewish people to arm and protect themselves and ordered that Haman be hung on his own gallows (Esther 3). To this day the Jewish people remember God's protection and Esther's courage during Purim.

Daniel

The book of Daniel shows another example of a person reaping a harvest of destruction from their corrupt seeds. Though taken from his homeland and forced to serve the king of Babylon, Daniel worked as unto the Lord and quickly became one of the king's most trusted advisors. However, other government officials grew jealous of Daniel's favor and devised a scheme to ensnare him. They drafted a decree that for thirty days no one should worship or pray to anyone human or divine except for the king (Dan. 6:7). If violated they would be thrown into the lion's den. Once the king signed the decree it became law and could not be changed. Daniel knew this but refused to honor man or man's laws above God. Daniel continued to practice his faith and pray to God openly. This is exactly what the corrupt government officials were counting on. That evening when Daniel returned to his home to pray, they were waiting in order to arrest Daniel and throw him into the lion's den. The king was devastated, but God miraculously protected Daniel through the whole night. The next morning when the king came to check on Daniel he was delighted to discover him still alive. He released Daniel and had the government officials who had made the evil plan along with their families thrown into the pit. They were immediately devoured and the king honored the God of Daniel (Dan. 6).

These scriptures also show us that not every negative harvest we experience in life is a result of seeds we've personally sown. Some experiences are the results of seed others have sown. While I'll look at this principle in greater detail in a later chapter (Reaping Where We Did Not Sow), I want to encourage you to consider the truth that we can sow to the future we desire. We do not have to be victims of circumstance. Instead, we can be victors through seedtime and harvest. Jesus wanted His followers to understand the importance of seeds. He taught:

So is the kingdom of God, as if a man should cast **seed** *into the* **ground**; *and should sleep, and rise night and day, and the seed should spring and grow up, he knoweth not how. For the earth bringeth forth fruit of* **herself**; *first the blade, then the ear, after that the full corn in the ear. But when the fruit is brought forth, immediately he putteth in the sickle, because the harvest is come.*

Mark 4:26-29(KJV)

Sowing and reaping expands God's Kingdom on earth. As co-laborers in His harvest field, we must understand how this principle translates in our lives (1 Cor. 3:6-9). To do so, let's look at two elements of this principle—seeds and ground. Seeds, both natural and spiritual, are full of life. The ground is an incubator. Like the womb of a woman, it produces fruit of itself. The King James Version of Mark 4 declares the earth brings forth fruit of **herself.** Together, these two components—seed and soil—have limitless potential to produce.

Manna, An Exceptional Case

In life, everything we need is waiting in the ground for a seed that will activate it and produce a harvest. For a time, God suspended this law during Israel's experience in the wilderness. For 40 years instead of needing to sow and reap, food fell from the sky. Scripture tells us that even their clothes and shoes did not wear out during this time (Deut. 29:5). God supernaturally provided for them. Yet when the Israelites entered the Promised Land, the manna ceased (Joshua 5:12) They no longer needed God's miraculous provision. The land (ground) provided all they would need and there would be a seed for every need.

Saints, though God does occasionally use miracles to work in our lives, the principle of sowing and reaping is His divine design. It is His plan for meeting our needs. Miracles bypass natural law. They cannot sustain us indefinitely. Seedtime and harvest can. From the beginning, God planned this:

> *Then God said, "Let the* **earth** *bring forth grass, the herb that yields* **seed***, and the fruit tree that yields fruit according to its kind, whose* **seed** *is in itself, on the earth;" and it was so. And the* **earth** *brought forth grass, the herb that yields* **seed** *according to its kind, and the tree that yields fruit, whose* **seed** *is in itself according to its kind. And God saw that it was good[...] And God said, "See, I have given you every herb that yields* **seed** *which is on the face of all the earth, and every tree whose fruit yields* **seed***; to you it shall be for food."*
>
> Genesis 1:11-12, 29

Incorruptible Seeds

Everything—and I mean everything—comes from seed that reproduces after its own kind—even you and me. (We beat out millions of other seeds in a race to unite with an egg from our mothers. We've been more than conquerors since conception!) That was our first birth (natural). Listen to what Peter says in 1 Peter 1:23: *"being born again, not of corruptible* **seed***, but of incorruptible, by the word of God, which liveth and abideth for ever"* (KJV). Our new birth experience came from the seed of God's Word (spiritual). To get corn, we plant a corn seed. To get wheat we plant wheat.

Lions, too, have seed. And that seed produces nothing but lions. Trout produce more trout. Monkeys produce only monkeys. The theory of evolution attempts to pervert or corrupt this law of nature by saying that with enough time one species, or seed, can produce a different species. That is wrong. There may be an evolution within a species to adapt to changing environments, but not from one species to another. A monkey cannot evolve into a human. That would violate God's law of sowing and reaping. Evolution is a seed of confusion and corruption sown by those who desire to cancel God's Word and their accountability to it. It brings us back to the admonition in Galatians 6:7, *"Be not deceived."* Yet Isaiah says:

> *"For my thoughts are not your thoughts, nor are your ways My ways," says the Lord. "For as the heavens are higher than the earth, so are My ways higher than your ways, and My thoughts than your thoughts. For as the rain comes down, and the snow from heaven, and do not return there, but water the earth, and make it bring forth and bud, that it may give* **seed to the sower** *and bread to the eater, so shall My word be that goes forth from My mouth; it shall not return to Me void, but it shall accomplish what I please, and it shall prosper in the thing for which I sent it."*
>
> Isaiah 55:8-11

God has rained His thoughts down one raindrop and snowflake at a time. Each of them like a seed to be sown into the heart, to blossom and bloom into a beautiful garden bringing God glory. The scriptures are God's thoughts and ways from heaven for our hearts in seed form. We can overcome deception through a knowledge and understanding of God's Word.

God's Word does not return to Him void. It is seed for the sower and food to the eater. Whether we sow it or feed upon it,

God's Word is never wasted. The life within it prospers. It reproduces after its own kind to transform our hearts and lives.

Mary

We can see this truth manifest in Mary's life when the angel Gabriel told her that she would conceive and give birth to the Son of God. (You can read the full account of this story in Luke chapter one.) When Mary first heard the news, she was perplexed. She asked, *"How is that possible? I've never known a man"* (vs. 34) Mary was not questioning God here. She simply asked a question. There is a difference. One stems from a heart of unbelief. The other seeks clarity so the hearer can obey. Mary knew that seed was required to have a baby. Since she was not married, and had never been intimate with a man, she didn't understand how she could fulfill the word of God. The angel, Gabriel, explained that the Holy Spirit would come upon Mary, and the seed of the word would bring about an immaculate conception: *"For with God nothing will be impossible"* (Luke 1:37).

Mary mixed faith with her word from God, and said, *"Let it be to me according to Your word"* (vs. 38). Immediately, the seed of God's word went to work. And nine months later, the greatest miracle to ever occur was born. God was made flesh. The Amplified Classic Translation (AMPC) of verse 37 adds, *"For with God nothing is ever impossible and no word from God shall be without power or impossible of fulfillment."* God's Word, like seed, is full of life and power. Once sown into a heart of faith, it cannot help but fulfill itself. This is what scripture means when it says that what God promises, He also performs (Rom. 4:21). But it takes partnership. It takes a believing heart to be good ground for that seed.

You cannot sow seeds on concrete and expect a harvest. It doesn't work in the natural realm, and it doesn't work in the spiritual realm either. The ground matters. This mystery of the ground may seem simplistic, but I assure you, it is profound. And while each of us understand this truth to a measure, most do not apply it to their walk with the Lord. In Mark 4:13-20, Jesus taught that there are four types of ground. He likened that ground to the human heart and described how each type partnered with the seed sown. I will expound on this concept in the next chapter, but for now know that only good ground yields a harvest—and the seed and ground must be watered to yield its potential and strength.

Water And Seed

Before Noah's flood, the earth had not experienced rain. The ground was watered from beneath its surface (Gen. 2:6). This is the same way the Holy Spirit waters the seed sown in our heart. In scripture, water is often a symbol of the work of the Holy Spirit. In Genesis, the Spirit of God hovered over the face of the waters (Gen. 1:2). In John 4:14 Jesus was sharing with the Samaritan woman at a well how life in the Spirit will quench our thirst, *"whoever drinks of the **water** that I shall give him will never thirst. But the **water** that I shall give him will become in him a fountain of **water** springing up into everlasting life."* In John 7:37-39 Jesus said, *"If anyone thirsts, let him come to Me and drink. He who believes in Me, as the Scripture has said, out of his heart will flow rivers of living **water**.' But this He spoke concerning the Spirit, whom those believing in Him would receive; for the **Holy Spirit** was not yet given, because Jesus was not yet glorified."* Notice how Jesus used water as a symbol of the work of the Holy Spirit. When we pray in the Spirit, living water flows from us to water God's Word from below the surface. Just like it did in Genesis. Let that sink in. Ezekiel spoke of living water coming out of the temple and bringing life everywhere it flowed (Ez. 47). Your born-again spirit has the Holy Spirit in it. Living water is in your spirit, springing up into your soul to water any seed you and

Jesus plant. This is what Jesus meant by, *"a fountain of water springing up into everlasting life"* (John 4:14).

This is why I don't understand people laboring to get the Word from their mind to their spirit. But Jesus is the Word (John 1:14). He is united to our spirit (1 Cor. 6:17). Christ is in us the Hope of Glory (Col. 1:27). We don't need to get God's Word into our spirits. He is already there. 1 Corinthians 2:16 says, *"For 'who has known the mind of the Lord that he may instruct him?' But we have the mind of Christ."* Did you get that? We have the mind of Christ! Where? In our spirit. In our spirit dwells all the hidden treasures of wisdom and knowledge (Col. 2:3). That is not true of our souls, which are still subject to sinful temptations, but in our spirits we house the Spirit of God.

1 John 2:20 says we have an anointing from the Holy One and we know all things. Yet, in that same chapter we are also told that, *"the same anointing teaches you concerning all things"* (vs. 27). So which is it? Both. In our born-again spirit we have the mind of Christ. We are united to Jesus and one spirit with the Lord (1 Cor. 6:17). We do know all things in our spirit man. But in our soul, we must be taught of the Spirit. That's why scripture admonishes us to renew our minds (Rom. 12:2). We are not renewing our spirit. It is already renewed in knowledge after the image of Him that created it, God (Col. 3:10). The transformation of our lives comes from the renewing of our minds (soul), not our spirits. Anointed speakers who water God's Word are drawing the waters from within to water the seed. You see, every seed planted in our soul must be watered from our spirit by the work of the Holy Spirit. So, when we sow God's Word in our hearts (souls), it is the Spirit from within that waters that seed causing it to take root. The revelation or understanding of that promise in seed form comes from within by the living water in our spirit man. The water under the ground waters the seed sown in the ground.

Another way the Spirit does this is through anointed teaching. 1 Corinthians 3:6 says, *"I planted, Apollos **watered**, but God gave the increase."* Paul was anointed to sow. Apollos was anointed to water what was sown by the same Spirit. But God gave the increase. God caused the seed to grow and produce fruit after it was watered by the Spirit. What we will learn shortly is that any harvest off that seed is credited to Jesus, the Lord of the harvest (Matt. 9:38). Notice again that it is the renewing of our minds, not the removing of them, that facilitates our transformation. We have to let the Holy Spirit nurture the seed of the Word so that our minds are renewed to His truth.

Death Of A Seed

Recently, two scientists in Israel, germinated a handful of 2,000-year-old seeds found in caves near the Dead Sea. The seeds are from an extinct date palm native to the Judean desert. In 2020, they harvested the first fruits from those trees and each year, their crop increases.[1] This amazing feat simply demonstrates another of the great mysteries of seeds. Seeds remain dormant until they are sown and die. Jesus explained this truth: *"I tell you the truth, unless a kernel of wheat is planted in the soil and **dies**, it remains alone. But its **death** will produce many new kernels—a plentiful harvest of new lives"* (John 12:24, NLT).

Seeds must die before they can produce a harvest. Only after a seed splits open and dies is the life within it revealed. Jesus, the Promised Seed, was a model of this truth (Gen. 3:19). His death produced a harvest of sons and daughters of the Kingdom. Unfortunately, many people have not understood this profound mystery. They never receive a harvest off their seeds sown

---

[1] https://www.youtube.com/watch?v=-3mMAvbcZf4&t=268s ;
https://www.science.org/content/article/dead-sea-dates-grown-2000-year-old-seeds

because they do not allow the seed to die. How does the seed die? It dies when we release it to God with no selfish motives. They do not release their seed to the Lord of the Harvest as a form of death.

Truly letting go of a seed after it is sown, means that seed dies to me. I cannot manipulate the harvest. I may sow in one person's life yet reap through another. I may sow into one ministry and reap from another. This is something I misunderstood for years. I'd sow a seed of kindness, and that person would turn on me. They would be anything but kind. I thought them being kind to me was my harvest, but I had an improper motive. I was kind so they would be kind in return. I was trying to manipulate my harvest and force my seed to come back through that person. But scripture teaches that I am to sow kindness to all regardless of their response (Matt. 5:44). While I can expect a harvest on each seed I sow, I can't control when or where I receive the harvest. That is in the Lord's hands; He is the Lord of the harvest.

The same is true in my giving. When I give, when I sow seed, that seed must die to me before it can produce in my life. I don't just give to get. I'm not giving to receive praise of men or even to be seen of men. If I'm giving just to get or be seen of men (impure motives), that seed never dies and the praise of men will be all I get (enjoy it while it lasts—Matt. 6:1). Nor do I give to earn or deserve something of God. When I give with these bad motives, the seed never dies. I give, knowing I will receive, so I can give again. By dying to the selfish motive of greed, I allow the life in my seed to produce a financial harvest in my life. Brothers and sisters, we must stop trying to manipulate our harvests. We can plant. We can expect a harvest on any seed we've sown, but we cannot predict nor control how that harvest appears in our life. How, when, or even where we reap is in the hands of the Lord of the harvest. Remember, *"I planted, Apollos watered, but God gave the increase [harvest]"* (1 Cor. 3:6). We are only in control of planting or watering; God has full control of the harvest.

To take this a step further, I can share the things of God, but He is the One who convicts, convinces, and converts. I can't convict anyone of sin; I can only pray for their hearts to be open. I can't convince anyone of truth; I can only speak the truth in love. I can't convert anyone to Christ; I can only introduce them to Jesus. In Acts chapter two, we see the believers in one accord. Every day they went to the temple and broke bread from house to house. And scripture says, *"the **Lord added** to the church daily those who were being saved"* (vs. 47). Notice that the Lord added to the church. My job, as part of the fivefold ministry, is to feed and lead the sheep. God builds the church (Jer. 3:15/ Matt. 16:18). I plant and water. But Jesus, as Lord of the Harvest, chooses how, where, and when the harvest comes. He gives the increase (1 Cor. 3:6).

Reaping A Harvest

Each of us have to learn the mysteries surrounding sowing *and* reaping. We also must understand the mysteries associated with this law to maximize our harvest. We have to learn to sow seed, release it to the Lord of the Harvest, and let it die, watching and resting in faith, patiently awaiting the harvest. Then, when we reap, we can turn around and sow again. Years ago, I struggled with this, especially in the area of finances. The Lord was faithful to bring about a harvest, but false humility kept me from reaping the full potential of my harvest. A wise farmer does not do that. A farmer understands the power of sowing, yes, but he must also discern when the harvest is ready and be willing to receive it. Though I was operating in the truth that "it is more blessed to give than receive," by not reaping when the Lord provided, I was robbing others of partaking in that same blessing (Acts 20:35/

John 15:8). I had to learn to put the sickle to the ground and reap my full harvest. Many crops have rotted in the fields because a lack of discernment kept God's people from reaping their harvest. Jesus taught:

> *The Kingdom of God is like a farmer who scatters seed on the ground. Night and day, while he's asleep or awake, the seed sprouts and grows, but he does not understand how it happens.* **The earth** *produces the crops on its own. First a leaf blade pushes through, then the heads of wheat are formed, and finally the grain ripens. And as soon as the grain is ready, the farmer comes and* **harvests it with a sickle***, for the harvest time has come.*
>
> Mark 4:26-29(NLT)

Seedtime

Another major element involved in our sowing and reaping is time. The mystery of time must be factored in order to patiently await your harvest. The lack of patience can hinder the full potential of the harvest. First the blade, then the ear, then the **full** corn in the ear. Don't harvest the blade or the ear, wait for the full corn in the ear. Hebrews 6:12 tells us that through faith and patience we inherit God's promises. Only through faith and patience (time) do we inherit (reap) the promises (fruit of the Kingdom). Though we all want instant results—except on any bad seeds we've sown—overnight harvests are rare. They would fall under the category of "miracle." 2 Corinthians 3:18 says, *"But we all, with unveiled face, beholding as in a mirror the glory of the Lord, are being transformed into the same image* **from glory to glory***, just as by the Spirit of the Lord."*. Notice that change is progressive. Growth is also progressive. Even in the natural world, different seeds grow at different rates and are ready for harvest on different timetables. Corn only takes a few months to grow from seed to harvest. An acorn takes years before we see a mature oak tree.

I have been in ministry a long time, and in that time, I've experienced both kinds of harvests. I've seen people receive the Word and experience change in just a few days. I've also planted churches that took years to develop healthy, lasting fruit. The same could be said of the seed planted in my own life. Once when pastoring in the Methodist church, a dear lady stopped me after service and said, "In ten years you're really going to be good." Ouch! Though I didn't appreciate her words at the time, her heart was right. She'd been enjoying the message and was attempting to bless me. She wasn't saying I was bad now, but that I should have hope for the future. She thought I was good then but would get even better over time. Like a good wine only becomes better with age and time, so was a young pastor going to be vintage wine in time (I believe, I receive!)

It takes time, and a lot of sowing, to reap sound character, integrity, and the ability to communicate well. My job, both then and now, is to keep sowing God's Word in my heart (to keep studying) and denying self (my old thought-life) as I trust the Lord of the Harvest to grow an ability within me to be a good communicator. I've been doing that for more than 40 years, and I believe I've gotten a bit better.

One Form to Another

Another reason we don't recognize when our harvest is ripe and ready for reaping is because we do not understand that seeds are often sown in one form and reaped in another. A further great mystery. 1 Corinthians 15:42-44 shares this principle as it relates to our bodies. It says our bodies are sown in corruption and raised in incorruption; sown in dishonor and raised in glory; sown in weakness, raised in power; sown natural, raised spiritual. Notice they are sown in one form and reaped in a different form.

I'm not suggesting we sow corn and reap apples. Seeds only reproduce after their own kind. But what if we sow an acorn and reap a baseball bat or a piano? Would we recognize it? We would have made the oak tree that grew from an acorn into a bat anyway. What if God, in His kindness, fast-forwarded those steps for us? Would we turn down His provision because it wasn't what we expected, but maybe it was even better? Think about it. What if we sowed apples and reaped apple juice? What if we sowed wheat and reaped a bakery? In each instance it is the same seed. It has reproduced after its own kind. But it was sown in one form and reaped in another. It was sown as a seed and reaped an expression of that seed's potential. Many people simply do not recognize the wonderful harvest reaped from precious seeds sown because of this concept of it being sown in one form and reaped in another.

We can see this truth in the life and death of Jesus. After His resurrection, two of His disciples were traveling on the road to Emmaus discussing Jesus' death and empty tomb. A man they did not recognize—Jesus in resurrected form—joined them. Jesus walked with them and explained how all that had happened to Him was in fulfillment of scripture. The disciples were amazed at His words, so they invited the man to dinner. (They still didn't know who He was.) As He ate with them, Jesus spoke His customary blessing over the bread and broke it. And scripture says, *"Their eyes were opened, and they knew Him"* (Luke 24:13-35). You see, Jesus was sown in one form and reaped in another. He was sown a single member body and reaped a many member body (1 Cor. 12:12-14). Do we recognize Him?

A similar experience happened to Mary Magdalene. She was one of the first to discover Jesus' empty tomb. But not understanding what it meant, she stood there weeping until angels appeared to comfort her. The angels spoke to her:

"Woman, why are you weeping?" She said to them, "Because they have taken away my Lord, and I do not know where they have laid Him." Now when she had said this, she turned around and saw Jesus standing there, and **did not know that it was Jesus.** *Jesus said to her, "Woman, why are you weeping? Whom are you seeking?" She,* **supposing Him to be the gardener,** *said to Him, "Sir, if You have carried Him away, tell me where You have laid Him, and I will take Him away." Jesus said to her, "Mary!" She turned and said to Him, "Rabboni!" (which is to say, Teacher).*

John 20:13-16

Mary thought Jesus was the gardener. She did not recognize Him for He had been sown in one form and reaped in another. Scripture tells us that Adam was the gardener of first creation (Gen. 2). Now we see Jesus, the Second Man, the last Adam, taking His place as the gardener of the New Creation (John 20:13-16; /1 Cor. 15:45, 47). Jesus was sown as a Son and risen as Lord of the Harvest. Now Jesus partners with us in the gardening of our hearts to produce a harvest off every good seed we sow. The gardener of the new creation is awesome! When we sow in one form, we now trust God to open our eyes to the harvest, even if it comes in another form.

In 2 Corinthians 9:6-8 we see this truth expressed in our giving. If we sow sparingly we reap sparingly, if bountifully we reap bountifully. Then we get to purpose how we sow cheerfully because God loves a cheerful giver. Then it says in verse 8— *"God is able to* **make all grace** *abound toward you, that you, always having all sufficiency in all things, may have an abundance for every good work."* Notice our giving heart in seed form (finances) released a harvest of "all grace abounding." Grace here in the Greek language is "Charis" and means favor (Strongs, charis-G5485). Cheerful, pure-heart giving is a seed sown in one form and reaped in another form—FAVOR. All grace (favor) and a harvest of favor is God's prosperity or harvest in our lives. It is God's favor in life that opens doors to true prosperity. God's favor will make you an attraction and magnet to others. People and finances will be drawn to you because of grace. You will no longer be seeking money; money will be seeking you. HALLELUJAH!

The prayer Paul prayed for the Ephesian believer applies here for our harvest, *"that the God of our Lord Jesus Christ, the Father of glory, may give unto you the spirit of* **wisdom** *and* **revelation** *in the knowledge of Him: the* **eyes of your understanding** *being enlightened; that ye may know what is the hope of his calling, and what the riches of the glory of His inheritance in the saints"* (Eph. 1:17-18 KJV).

My prayer for you is that God would open your eyes to the wonderful harvest regardless of its form.

Chapter 3

The Ground

*For the earth bringeth forth fruit of **herself**; first the blade, then the ear, after that the full corn in the ear.*

Mark 4:28, KJV

Most of us have been taught that plants and animals come from seeds, which is true and something I just shared as well. However, consider this mystery: seeds are worthless without good ground. This may seem simplistic, but I assure you it is profound. As we've seen, seeds remain dormant until they fall to the ground and die (John 12:24). But scripture also speaks of the role of the ground or earth, saying that the earth yields fruit "of herself" (Mark 4:28 KJV). How is this possible? The earth is feminine (Mother Earth comes to mind). Like a womb, earth only requires seed to activate its power to produce.

Seed without a womb is useless and a womb without seed is barren. They work together. But, originally, everything came from the ground. All the gold, silver, steel, iron, oil, and any other resource you can name came from the ground in original creation. Everything above ground was below the ground first. Let that sink in for a moment. Genesis two says, *"And out of the* **ground** *the Lord God made every tree grow [...]out of the* **ground** *the Lord formed every beast of the field and every bird of the air* (vs. 9, 19). Everything—every plant, tree, bird, and animal—even Adam came from the ground (Gen. 2:7). So the answer to, "which came first, the chicken or the egg?" is simple: the chicken! The chicken came from the ground with the capacity to reproduce (eggs) after its own kind.

Everything we need is in the ground. Corn, apples, and watermelons are all in the ground. Trees and flowers are as well and all it takes is a seed to activate each one. Now I realize this mystery may seem foreign to many people. Most of our science classes did not do a good job of sharing biblically accurate information, and not always for nefarious reasons. Human knowledge is simply limited. It only comes from natural observation and experimentation. But science eventually catches up with the Word of God over time.

Take, for example, science's understanding of space. At one time science claimed the earth was the center of our fixed universe. Now we know the sun is the center of our galaxy and our galaxy is one of millions in an expanding universe. This corresponds with the prophets saying that God stretches out the heavens and that He created the number of stars and knows them each by name (Is. 40:22-26, 42:5). Or consider how recent scientific studies have improved agriculture. We know now (and are teaching other nations) the importance of crop rotation or land rest and soil amendments. Yet the Word of God has always declared these things. That is why Israel rested the land every seven years (Lev. 25:4). It is why Jesus could use the parable of the sower to teach about the condition of men's hearts. His audience understood that different types of soils would respond differently to seed (Mk 4 / Matt 13).

In original creation, everything came from the ground with seed in it for reproducing: *"And God said, 'See I have given you every herb that **yields seed** which is on the face of all the earth, and every tree whose **fruit yields seed**; to you it shall be for food* (Gen. 1:29). The ground bore fruit and the fruit yielded seed. In time, that seed returned to the ground to activate more fruit carrying more seed. Even mankind came that way. *"And the Lord God formed man of the dust of the **ground**, and breathed into his nostrils the breath of life"* (Gen. 2:7). Adam came out of the ground bearing seed and was eventually returned to it (as all of us are according to Gen 3:19/Ps. 104:29/Ecc. 3:20). We see this truth of the power and potential of the ground illustrated in the story of Cain and Abel. Moses records this account in Genesis chapter 4.

Cain

Genesis 4:2 says, *"Abel was a keeper of sheep, but Cain was a **tiller of the ground**."* Cain is following in the vocation of his father Adam. He works the ground and is a gardener. Verses 3-4 say *"and in the process of time it came to pass that Cain brought an offering of the **fruit of the ground** to the Lord. Abel also brought of the first born of his flock and of their fat."* Notice the ground is producing fruit of itself or herself. The seeds he sowed activated the ground to produce. Abel offered up the firstborn of his flock, a more excellent offering and the Lord receives Abel's offering and rejects Cain's. Cain is angered by this and out of jealous rage kills Abel, his brother. God confronts Cain over his sin and declares the consequences of his horrific action.

Genesis 4:10-12 says *"What have you done? The voice of your brother's blood cries out to me **from the ground**. So now you are cursed from the **earth**, which has opened its mouth to receive your brother's blood from your hand. When you till the ground, it **shall no longer yield its strength** to you."* Wow! In verse 2, before Cain's sin, the earth yielded its strength to him and produced a harvest. After his sin it no longer yielded its strength. Every time Cain sowed a seed, the ground rejected it. It cried out, "what you did was wrong." It was the ground that cursed Cain, not God! This earth was originally created in righteousness and holiness and even seedtime and harvest looked different then, compared to what we see today. Sin in our world has affected everything including the ground. 2 Chronicles 7:14 *"if my people who are called by My name will humble themselves, and pray and seek My face, and turn from their wicked ways, then I will hear from heaven, and will forgive their sin and* **heal their land** *[ground]."*

Israel's sins affected the land. Their repentance brought healing to the land. I'm convinced had Cain repented, God would have healed the land (the ground), and Cain would have prospered. The ground would have once again produced of herself (yielded her strength). It would have blessed Cain again rather than curse; yielding of herself versus withholding.

Thousands of years later the prophet Malachi recorded what life in covenant with God would look like: *"'Bring all the tithes into the storehouse, that there may be food in My house, and try me now in this,' says the Lord of hosts, 'If I will not open for you the windows of heaven and pour out for you such blessing that there will not be room enough to receive it. And I will rebuke the devourer for your sakes, so that he will not destroy the fruit of your* **ground***, Nor shall the vine fail to bear fruit for you in the field'"* (Mal. 3:10-11). The blessing of the tithe (first fruits) continues under the New Testament. Our covenant is a better covenant. Under the New Testament we have authority to rebuke Satan and receive blessing and healing for our ground to produce fruit, which includes our heart, as good ground. Sin affected the ground and now righteousness does as well. A day is coming, dear ones, when the children of God will inherit a new land—a new heaven and earth wherein nothing but righteousness will dwell.

We will all receive our new resurrected immortal bodies, and the earth will return to its original state of righteousness and holiness.

We see in the New Testament the effects of sin on the earth:

> *For the earnest expectation of the creation eagerly waits for the revealing of the sons of God. For the creation was subjected to futility, not willingly, but because of Him who subjected it in hope; because the creation itself also will be delivered from the bondage of corruption into the glorious liberty of the children of God. For we know that the whole creation groans and labors with birth pangs together until now.*
>
> Romans 8:19-22

Adam's sin subjected the earth to the curse of the fall (not law) unwillingly. Just like Cain's sin affected the ground and Israel's sins affected the land, our sins are affecting the earth. The planet rests in hope for the day we are manifested as the sons and daughters of God. We are that now, but we have not been fully manifested and revealed as the sons and daughters of God. There is a new heaven and a new earth (ground) coming at the appearing of Jesus and His kingdom. The church will receive our resurrected bodies, and the earth will return to her original state of righteousness and holiness. There will be no more sin and she will yield her full strength again. I can't wait to see the law of sowing and reaping in the new heaven and earth. Until that day, let's remember our covenant. Let's plant seeds knowing they will produce a harvest for our future. Let's partner with Jesus, the Lord of the Harvest, to guard and garden our hearts.

Our Hearts

Proverbs 4:23 *"keep your heart with all diligence, for out of it spring the issues of life."* Keep means guard in the Hebrew. In Genesis 2:15 we see Adam's assignment in the garden, *"Then the Lord took the man and put him in the garden of Eden to **tend** and **keep** it."* The King

James Version says, *"dress it and keep it."* Dress means to "work it or till" (Strongs—Aw-bad—H5647). Keep means to "guard, protect, attend to" (Strongs—shaw-mar—H8104). In other words, everything you need is in this ground awaiting a seed to activate it. So, work it, tend to it, and till it, making sure to protect and guard it the whole time. The ground cannot discern between good and evil. It cannot discriminate against any seed, so guard it, protect it. It will produce whatever is planted good or bad. Our hearts are the same. We must guard what seed we allow to be planted in our hearts. We are told in Proverbs 4:23 to guard our hearts for everything we need is in our ground. Every issue of our life is in our heart awaiting seed. Watch what seed you sow in your ground because it does not discriminate against any seed. Weeds activate a bad harvest. Good seeds activate a good harvest. You must determine what gets sown because the heart can't protect itself and Satan won't. Guard your heart, your ground, for out of it springs life's issues. Everything above ground in our lives came from below the ground of our hearts. Just like everything above ground in our world, came from below the ground of the earth.

Jesus In Biology and Seeds

Matthew 13:24-25 tells us *"the kingdom of heaven is like a man who sowed good **seed** in his field; but while men slept, his enemy came and sowed tares among the wheat and went his way."* Notice that the enemy (Satan) attacks the man by sowing bad seed in his field. This is why you must guard your field (heart). Jesus will partner with us to garden our hearts, but we have to choose to guard it. Jesus goes on to teach another parable in Matthew 13:31-32, *"The kingdom of heaven is like a mustard seed, which a man took and sowed in his field, which indeed is the least of all the **seeds**; but when it is grown it is greater than the herbs and becomes a tree, so that the birds of the air come and nest in its branches."* In both parables the word for seed in the Greek is SPERMA

(Strongs G4690) and refers to something sown that is seed (including the male sperm). This word for seed occurs 44 times in the New Testament. All the human heart needs in order to produce fruit is seed. Life is in the seed of God's Word to produce after its own kind when sown into the womb of our hearts. It will activate the Kingdom in our hearts and we will bear fruit, much like women bearing children (John 15:1-5,8). Remember Mark 4:28 KJV, *"For the earth bringeth forth fruit of **herself**."* Scripture uses this feminine imagery to show the potential for creating life that we have when our hearts mix with the seed of God's Word. Jesus often used this imagery of biology and the science of creation to convey the spiritual law of seeds sown in good ground.

A Blind Man

An excellent example of this mystery of the ground is found in John 9:1-7. Let me encourage you to read this story from a new understanding of seed and ground. In short, a man was born blind, and Jesus heals him. How? He spat on some clay (ground) and put it on the man's eyes and told him to go and wash in the pool of Siloam, which is by interpretation, Sent. The man mixed faith obedience with the word of Jesus and was healed. Remember, God created Adam (and all his organs) from the ground. Jesus is Creator God of all creation. Adam, the first man, came from the ground. All his organs, including his eyes, came from the ground. The first two original eyes came from the ground and were created by Jesus. Jesus, once again as Creator God, uses the ground (clay) to create new eyeballs for the blind man. His obedience was the faith seed used, and the water was the pool of Siloam. Our hearts are the ground for the seed of God's Word and the Holy Spirit is the one SENT by the Father to water the ground and seed bringing forth fruit. What a great mystery!

Everything we need in this life is available now in seed form in God's Word. It simply needs a heart that fears God so it can take root and bear fruit. You are that good ground awaiting the precious seed. While many people allow their past failures to sabotage their futures, you can break that cycle. You can repent of the negative seeds and subsequent harvests of the past. You can begin sowing good seeds and trust, that with Jesus as the Gardener of your heart, you will reap a glorious harvest off those seeds.

Chapter 4

Faith as a Seed

For assuredly, I say to you, if you have faith as a mustard seed, you will say to this mountain, 'Move from here to there,' and it will move; and nothing will be impossible for you.

Matthew 17:20b

What is God's Kingdom like? How does faith work in that kingdom? Jesus said it was like a mustard seed (Mark 4:30-32). Mustard seeds are exceedingly small. Yet they yield huge harvests. Jesus uses this comparison to create a picture in His hearers' minds. He wants us to recognize the Kingdom principle that small things can produce great harvests when sown by faith. Our faith is not the size of a mustard seed, but mustard seed faith is all we need to see miracles. It only takes a little faith to yield a huge harvest. Never doubt how so little can change so much.

Little Boy's Lunch

In Mark 6, thousands of people came to hear Jesus speak and be healed by Him. (This same story is recorded in Matthew 14 and Luke 9.) The people were so enthralled by His words that they stayed all day. Toward evening, when the people were hungry, Jesus told His disciples to feed them. The disciples were overwhelmed. They didn't have enough money to feed everyone, and the only food they could find was one little boy's lunch. Feeding such a multitude would be impossible! But Jesus didn't expect them to meet the need themselves. *"How many loaves do you have?"* He asked (Mark 6:38). And you know the rest of the story. Jesus took the five loaves and two fish in that little boy's lunch and fed over 5,000 men (not including women and children) with 12 baskets left over! All Jesus needed was a seed.

God has given each of us a seed to meet every need. All we have to do is mix faith with what we have and trust the Lord of the Harvest to turn that seed into a bountiful harvest—a harvest with enough to meet our need and extra to sow again. This is how we live in perpetual blessing (2 Cor. 9:10).

We've all been given seed to sow. But often, we feel like Jesus' disciples, overwhelmed by an impossible situation. We view our need as an immovable mountain and instead of looking for our little boy's lunch—our seed—we look around and focus on our need instead of discovering our seed. That is not productive. Or maybe we think our seed cannot withstand the winds of adversity to produce a harvest. Let me assure you that they can. They are vigorous and robust.

The only living things to survive the flood (that weren't on the ark) were seeds. When the rain stopped and Noah finally saw the waters receding, he sent birds out to find dry land. Eventually a dove returned with an olive leaf in its beak and Noah knew it was time to leave the ark. He knew there was enough food available for the survival of his family and all the animals (Gen. 6-9). Think about that. The earth had protected the seeds of every plant God created so that as soon as the sun touched the ground, those seeds began producing. They may have lain dormant for a time, but their life did not diminish. The same is true of the seeds we sow. Even those sown in adversity are still there. They are simply waiting for a tiny "mustard seed" of faith to signal that the ground of our heart is ready for the light of Jesus to shine upon it. They will bring forth fruit, fruit enough to meet our need and give us something to sow again to meet someone else's need.

We should never despise seeds—no matter how small. Seeds can change the course of our life. James talks about this. He reminds his hearers that small bits control huge horses (James 3:3). Small rutters turn massive ships (vs. 4). And even a single match can burn down thousands of acres (vs. 5). James says the human tongue is the same. Though small, it sets the course of our lives (vs. 6). The writer of Proverbs 18 agrees: *"Death and life are in the power of the tongue, and those who love it will eat its fruit"* (vs. 21).

Notice the connection between these comparisons. Our words are like seeds that produce a harvest in our lives. Whether those seeds are good or bad will determine the type of fruit we bear and "eat." I meet people every day who think small things like words don't matter. That is not what scripture teaches.

A small seed from God's Word, when mixed with faith, can turn a life around. It can release an abundance of blessings. Never underestimate small things, even if that "small" thing is you. God excels at—and delights in—making small things great. Jesus was born in the small town of Bethlehem (Micah 5:2). Gideon, though of Isarel's weakest clan and the least in his father's house, delivered his people from the hand of the Midianites (Judges 6-8). Jeremiah, too, began his ministry with a feeling of insignificance. He called himself a "youth" who couldn't speak. But God corrected him. He told Jeremiah, "Don't say that." In other words, "Jeremiah, your words are important. Use them wisely." Then God touched Jeremiah's mouth and put His words within it (Jer. 1:7). He sent Jeremiah to the nations (Jer. 1:4-10)! If we're going to fulfill God's plan for our lives, like Jeremiah, we need to learn to respond to God's Word in faith. We need to learn to say what God says.

Widow Of Zarephath

In 1 Kings 17, evil King Ahab is worshipping idols and teaching the Israelites to do the same. The prophet Elijah calls for a drought to get his attention, and later he faces the effects of that drought. God sends Elijah to the brook Cherith and supernaturally provides for him there. Eventually, those provisions run out, so God instructs Elijah to go to Zarephath where He has spoken to a widow to provide for the prophet. This information is important to understand Elijah's next actions.

When he arrives, Elijah sees a woman (widow) gathering sticks for a fire. He asks her for a drink and a piece of bread. The woman replies, "I don't have anything to spare. I'm gathering these sticks to make a final meal for my son and myself before we die." Elijah tells her, "Give me the food first" (vs. 12-13, paraphrased). Most people freak out about that, wondering how Elijah could be so selfish, but remember, Elijah knows God had spoken to a widow. The widow knows she is to provide for a prophet. Both are mixing faith with the word God gave them. They are each looking for the other. Keep this in mind when Elijah tells her to feed him first. Elijah knew that if this woman ate the last of her flour and oil, it would truly be her last meal. But if she mixed faith with it as a seed, she would reap more than enough to eat and sow again. Elijah prophesies to the woman that her flour and oil would not be used up until the Lord sends rain to end the drought. The woman did as Elijah asked, and the word of the Lord proved true.

Her faith, as a mustard seed, was more than enough. Mixing faith with so little produced so much.

A Widow with Two Sons

Years later, Elisha, the successor of Elijah, experienced a similar miracle. In 2 Kings four, a widow with two sons is facing insurmountable debt. Creditors are coming to take her sons as indentured servants until the debt is paid. Children who could work were considered collateral on unpaid debts. She asks Elisha for help, and Elisha asks, "What do you have?" In other words, where is your seed? The woman replies, "I have nothing but a jar of oil" (vs. 2, paraphrased).

Elisha tells her to borrow as many pots as she can find and pour her oil into them. The woman follows the prophet's instructions in faith obedience and fills every pot in the house. She sells the oil, pays the debt, and has enough left over that she and her sons can live off the rest. What a beautiful picture of sowing and reaping. As long as the woman poured the oil, which is symbolic of giving, she continued to reap a harvest. She didn't run out of oil until she ran out of pots or places to sow. I imagine, in hindsight, she wished she had borrowed more pots!

You see, dear ones, we can mix faith with anything and make it a seed. Look at this verse from Luke 6:38. *"Give, and it will be given to you: good measure, pressed down, shaken together, and running over will be put into your bosom. For with the same measure that you use, it will be measured back to you."* Ministers often use this verse to encourage people to give offerings. And while this principle certainly applies to money, notice that money is never mentioned here. It simply says to give. That giving could be anything. Kindness. Mercy. Time. A car. Literally anything can become a seed when it is mixed with faith and given in love.

Cana Wedding

In the second chapter of John, Jesus is invited to a wedding in Cana. While there, a need is brought to His attention. The wine had run out, which was inexcusable and embarrassing for the hosts. Jesus instructs the servants to fill six pots with water. They obey and Jesus sends them to the master of the feast with a cup drawn from the pots. On their way, the water turns into wine—but not just any wine, the best wine of the feast. Now I don't want you to miss the significance of Jesus' actions here. In every miracle Jesus performed, He first looked for a seed. Our focus must always shift from need to seed. Jesus mixed faith with that seed and trusted God for the harvest. He mixed faith with pots of water to create pots of wine. It was sown in one form and reaped in another.

We often tend to dismiss the things Jesus did as simply acts of His divinity. But Jesus is the pattern-Son. He didn't perform miracles on this earth as Son of God (deity). He performed them as Son of Man (humanity). That is not to say that Jesus' miracles did not point to His identity as God's Son. They did. They also showed us what God was really like. But the way Jesus performed miracles was for our benefit. It gave us an example of how we, as sons and daughters of God, can believe and receive from God.

Many people do not believe we can see miracles today because they believe only Jesus could do those things since He was God. It is true that He was God, but God made flesh. He operated as a man in submission to God. He did what He did as an example for us to follow. It was Jesus who said, *"Verily, verily, I say unto you, He that believeth on me, the works that I do shall he do also; and* **greater works** *than these shall he do; because I go unto my Father"* (John 14:12 KJV). Jesus went unto the Father and the Father sent the Holy Spirit so we could see and do the supernatural.

Faith As A Seed

The seedtime and harvest principle worked quickly and perfectly in Jesus' life. But we're still learning and growing. Jesus saw seedtime as one word. He was able to apply this principle to the needs He encountered and see an immediate harvest. For most of us, this principle works more like seed . . . t–i–m–e . . . and harvest. The growing season takes a while. But praise God, the principle still works. We may not have arrived at seedtime and harvest, but we can head in that direction. We can start believing God and see the harvest on our seeds produce in shorter and shorter amounts of time.

Don't be deceived into thinking that if you had "more faith" you could speed up this process or that you need more faith. None of us need more faith. We have enough. We simply need to act on the faith we have. In Luke 17 Jesus encourages His disciples to forgive regardless of the frequency of offense or level of injury we experience. Their response amazes me. They had already been commanded to heal the sick, cleanse the leper, and raise the dead. But when Jesus told them to forgive, they said, "Lord, increase our faith" (Luke 17:5). They didn't ask for more faith to do miracles, just more faith to forgive. Notice Jesus' answer. I'm sure it surprised them just as much as it surprises people today. *"If you have faith* **as a mustard seed**, *you could say to this mulberry tree, Be pulled up by the roots and be planted in the sea,' and it would obey you"* (vs. 6). Jesus did not tell the disciples they needed more faith. Neither did He say their faith was mustard seed sized faith. Rather, He said it doesn't take much faith to see His power work. We simply need to act on the faith we have.

If we are born-again, we have the faith of Christ. Galatians 2:20 declares, *"I am crucified with Christ: nevertheless I live; yet not I, but Christ liveth in me: and the life which I now live in the flesh I live* **by the**

faith of the Son of God*, who loved me, and gave himself for me"* (KJV). Our faith is not too little. It is more than enough! When scriptures refer to great faith, little faith, etc., it's not referring to the amount or kind of faith we have, but rather how we're acting on and in it. The faith we have is the faith of Jesus! We all have the same measure and kind (Rom. 12:3).

Unbelief

When a man brought his demon-possessed son to Jesus' disciples, the disciples could not cast the demon out. So, the man brought his son to Jesus. Jesus called the disciples *"faithless and perverse"* and delivered the boy (Matt. 17:17). Jesus said they were being faithless and perverse. He didn't say they had "little" faith, He said they had none! Afterward the disciples ask why they couldn't cast the demon out, and Jesus said, *"Because of your unbelief"* (Matt. 17:20). Jesus went on to tell the disciples they didn't need big faith to do the impossible. All they needed was pure faith. Faith as a mustard seed—if not diluted with doubt and unbelief—is enough to move mountains.

When scripture refers to people with great or little faith it is not quantifying the amount of faith they have, but the amount of faith they are operating in. In Mark's account of this event Jesus asks the man if he believed Jesus could cast the demon out. The man replied, *"Lord, I believe; help my unbelief"* (vs. 9:24). It is possible to have faith and unbelief at the same time. But the net result is always zero. They cancel one another out. In Deuteronomy 22:9 God tells Israel not to mix seeds in their fields, *"lest the yield…be defiled."* This truth has not changed. The seed of faith does not mix well with the seed of unbelief. It becomes defiled. James 2:20 says that faith without works, or action, is dead. Some people's mountain-moving faith is unfruitful because they act out of fear and unbelief instead of faith. We need to learn to believe only so we can act on the faith we have. We don't have a faith problem; we have an unbelief problem. We need to believe only and doubt not in our heart. Jesus tells us in Mark 11:23 (KJV), *"That whosoever shall say unto this mountain, Be thou removed, and be thou cast into the sea; and* **shall not doubt** *in his heart, but shall believe that those things which he saith shall come to pass; he shall have whatsoever he saith."* Earlier in Jesus' ministry, He was heading to a ruler of the synagogue's home (Jairus) to heal his daughter. While on the way, word came to them that she had died. When Jesus heard those words (seeds) He looked at Jairus and told him to not be afraid but to only believe. Jesus was encouraging Jairus to not mix the seed of unbelief with his seed of faith but to only believe (Mark 5:35-36).

If you are battling unbelief, know there is a cure! I have an entire series that goes into detail about this subject. It's titled "Kinds of Unbelief," and is available for free download on my website. I'll share that teaching, in a nutshell, here, but I encourage you to listen to it in its entirety. You'll be blessed. Jesus went on to say in Matthew 17:21, *"However, this kind does not go out except by prayer and fasting."* Jesus was not referring to casting the demon out, but rather their unbelief. We do not have to pray and fast to cast demons out. No other scripture bears witness to that thinking. The prayer and fasting refers to casting out this type of unbelief that dominates so many Christians today. There are different kinds of unbelief that have a different cures to deal with them. Let's look at them and their cures.

Rejection of Jesus

The first kind of unbelief is the rejection of Jesus. This is the unpardonable sin—the only sin not covered by the cross of Christ. It is what the Holy Spirit convicts the world of:

> *And when He has come [The Holy Spirit], He will convict the world of sin, and of righteousness, and of judgment: of sin, because **they do not believe** in Me.*
>
> John 16:8-9

Notice that it is sin singular, not plural (sins). There is only one sin that was not covered on the cross and that is the rejection of the cross. We have to accept what Jesus did for us by faith to be saved. This is the sin against the Holy Spirit that will not be forgiven. *"Therefore I say to you, every sin and blasphemy will be forgiven men, but the blasphemy against the Spirit will **not be forgiven** men"* (Matt. 12:31). Rejecting the conviction of the Spirit of who Jesus is and the work of the cross is blaspheming the Holy Spirit. This kind of unbelief dominates the world and faith in Jesus is the cure.

Jesus is the only way of salvation. Only He was qualified to take our place on the cross, to bear God's wrath and the punishment for our sin. There is no other savior or sacrifice for our sins. There is no alternative for those who reject the provision offered us in Christ. But the cure for this unbelief is simple. All we have to do is believe in Jesus and His sacrifice for our sins on the cross and receive (Mark 16:16). To be delivered from this unbelief, we must have faith in who Jesus is and what He did in His death, burial, and resurrection. Romans says that if we believe that God raised Jesus from the dead, and confess Him as Lord, we are saved (Rom. 10:9-10). We are cured of this form of unbelief.

Lack of Knowledge

The second form of unbelief is a lack of knowledge. Much of the unbelief in the Church comes from a lack of knowledge of God's Word. Hosea 4:6 says, *"My people are destroyed for lack of knowledge."* But again, the cure is simple. It just takes time. We have to study God's Word. Romans says that faith comes by hearing God's Word (10:17). And 2 Peter says that grace and peace are multiplied to us through the **knowledge of God** (vs. 1:2). We cannot believe what we do not know. But faith—knowing God (not knowing about Him but of Him)—begins and ends with a knowledge of His Word. We are being delivered daily from this kind of unbelief as we submit to and hear God's Word.

Akin to a lack of knowledge is wrong knowledge. Many people's unbelief is rooted in lies, lies about God, themselves, and others. When people believe a lie it ensnares and enslaves them to unbelief. They believe, but believing a lie is unbelief. It cancels out "believe only." The cure for this unbelief is the "TRUTH" (John 8:31-32). Knowing the truth sets us free. Free from what? Lies and the snare of unbelief. In John 17:17 Jesus declares His word as truth, *"Sanctify them through thy truth: thy word is truth"* (KJV). God's Word is the truth that when known separates us from this form of unbelief.

Carnality

The third kind of unbelief is what the disciples dealt with—carnality. Carnal simply means five senses driven. Unbelief believes what we see, hear, smell, taste or touch more than God's Word. It walks by sight and not by faith. The disciples knew Jesus could cast the demon out of the boy in Matthew 17. They didn't doubt God or His ability. They doubted their ability. The disciples saw the boy demonstrate a fit of epilepsy. They saw him fall to the ground and foam at the mouth. Though God had used them to cast out demons before this event, they allowed their senses—what they could see, hear, smell, taste, or touch—to inspire unbelief (Luke 10:17). Jesus was clear in answering their question on why they couldn't do it. It was because of their unbelief, period. It wasn't that this demon was any stronger than the others they had cast out. It was the unbelief that comes from being dominated by our senses. Being carnally minded versus spiritually minded.

Our feelings are often dominated by our five physical senses, but allowing those senses free reign will produce unbelief in our hearts. Senses are carnal, not evil, but of the flesh, unreliable. When not under control they can lead to sin and unbelief (Rom. 8:7). Jesus said the cure for this kind of unbelief was fasting and prayer (Mark 9:28-29). Fasting and prayer teaches us to walk by faith instead of by sight (2 Cor. 5:7). It helps us develop relationship with God and learn to control our emotions. Fasting and prayer do not cast out demons. They cast out unbelief so that our seed of faith is not defiled. Prayer and fasting discipline our flesh and heighten our spiritual senses. The whole purpose of prayer and fasting is not to change God or intimidate Satan, but rather refine our hearts to believe only, changing us to doubt not in our hearts. Fasting and prayer will not earn us some special power to cast out demons, but they will cast out this kind of unbelief. This kind of unbelief is common among Christians, and we need the Holy Spirit to bring us conviction in this area. What's more real and going to dominate our lives—the natural or the spiritual? What are our five physical senses telling us or what does God's Word tell us? When we "believe only" we see God's power and our faith work.

Chapter 5

Faith Speaks

And since we have the same spirit of faith, according to what is written, "I believed and therefore I spoke," we also believe and therefore speak.

2 Corinthians 4:13

We've seen that faith works in our lives as a seed. But according to 2 Corinthians four, that seed is sown through our words. We believe and therefore we speak. Faith speaks, and so does doubt. Jesus said that out of the abundance of our hearts, our mouth speaks (Matt. 12:34). So whatever seeds are planted in our hearts in abundance will flow out of our heart through our words. So, words are seeds.

When my oldest daughter was in kindergarten, I picked her up from school one day and listened to her sing me a new song she had learned that day. Her version went something like this:

"Peanut sittin on a railroad track, his heart was full of butter.

He didn't hear the 5:16. TOOT! TOOT! Peanut butter."

[NOTE: This is how she sang it to me and how I've preached it.]

I knew it wasn't a country music song, even though it had a train and crisis involved. I hadn't heard it at church, either, but enjoyed her singing to me. The original version may be different as well, but it was her song and my joy and pleasure to listen.

She loved those last lines. She'd drag out the final words of each for dramatic effect (pea----nut but----ter). It was cute. Then, the powerful message of that little children's song struck me. Whatever our hearts are full of will come out when trials, tribulations, and trouble hits. What's in our hearts? Jesus gave us the indicator—our words. In time our words will show the true condition of our hearts. The approaching train will bring out what is really in there, not what we pretend is in there, or even hope is in there.

In Matthew chapter 12, Jesus answered the pharisees accusation that He was casting out demons and performing miracles by the power of Beelzebub. Jesus told them to examine His fruit, then went on to speak about the power of our words. In verses 34 and 35 He says, *"How can you, being evil, speak good things? For out of the abundance of the heart the mouth speaks. A good man out of the good treasure of his heart brings forth good things, and an evil man out of the evil treasure brings forth evil things."* Then He warns them, *"But I say to you that for every idle word men may speak, they will give account of it in the day of judgment. For by your words you will be justified, and by your words you will be condemned"* (vs. 36-37).

Wow. In the day of judgement, we will all give an account for every idle word we have spoken. How can an honest person look at scripture and say words don't matter? Words are powerful seeds that produce an eternal harvest of condemnation or justification. Want some good news? We get to choose which seeds we sow. And those seeds will reproduce after their own kind. Through repentance and forgiveness we can cancel out any bad seeds we sow. In God's mercy we can believe for "crop failure." What kind of life do you want in a year? In five years? What seeds are you sowing? Your life will follow the trajectory of the dominant seeds you sow. Sow wisely and with intention.

Proverbs is full of wisdom about this subject. Proverbs 15:4 says, *"A wholesome tongue is a **tree** of life, but perverseness in it breaks the spirit."* Notice the connection of our tongue with a tree. Our words are seeds that produce a tree of health and life if we sow them wisely. Proverbs 16:24 says, *"Pleasant words are like a honeycomb, sweetness to the soul and health to the bones."* Again, see how words affect our health, in both body and soul. Choose sweet words of life and not bitter words of death. Proverbs 18:20-21 says, *"A man's stomach shall be satisfied from the **fruit** of his mouth; from the produce of his lips he shall be filled. Death and life are in the power of the tongue, and those who love it will eat its **fruit**."* Our words are seeds of death or life and we will eat the fruit they produce. Our natural bellies are satisfied with the fruit of our hands (labor). Here, the stomach or belly represents our spirit man. Proverbs 20:27 says, *"The spirit of man is the candle of the Lord, searching all the inward parts of the belly"* (KJV). So many believers and unbelievers alike have missed this mystery and are reaping a negative harvest unwittingly. Our spirits are either satisfied or grieved by our words. Some people totally overlook this truth to their own demise, while others are totally deceived thinking their words don't matter. It is important we remember that God will not be mocked; seeds of death will never produce a harvest of life. And Proverbs 21:23 says, *"Whoever guards his mouth and tongue keeps his soul from troubles."* Notice how the tongue is connected to a life of blessing or brokenness, trouble or sweetness. Notice, too, that our words feed our belly or spirit man. (Prov. 20:27 uses these two words interchangeably.) Words are a seed whose byproduct can bring health or death. For though our natural food comes from the fruit of our hands, our spiritual food comes from the fruit of our lips.

Ever heard the saying "Sticks and stones may break my bones, but words can never hurt me?" That is a lie. Words are powerful. They can be wielded to heal or used as weapons of harm and hurt. Isaiah 54:17 declares, *"No weapon formed against you shall prosper, and* **every tongue** *which rises against you in judgment you shall condemn. This is the heritage of the servants of the Lord, and their righteousness is from Me,' says the Lord."* Words formed against us are weapons that must be condemned, not received. We do not condemn people, but we do reject the evil seeds of the tongue.

Words can also be weapons against the enemy. Jesus said His words were spirit and life (John 6:63). His words carried so much life they brought death to things that were contrary to God's will. His words destroyed darkness, sickness, and disease. Our words can be just as powerful if we use them wisely and properly. This is how Jesus did warfare with Satan on the mountain of temptation. In Matthew 4:4,7, &10 Jesus countered Satan's assaults on Him with the mighty phrase: *"It is written."* He spoke God's Word and bombed Satan off the mountain.

Jesus modeled the power of words when He cursed the fig tree in Mark chapter 11. On His way to Jerusalem, Jesus saw a fig tree outside Bethany. Though it wasn't the season for figs, the tree was leafed out. Jesus was hungry and went to investigate. But the tree bore no figs. Jesus cursed the tree saying, *"Let no one eat fruit from you ever again,"* (verse 14). At first, it appeared as though nothing happened. Twenty-four hours later, though, Jesus and the disciples passed by the tree again, returning from their journey. Peter noticed it had dried up from the roots. He remembered Jesus' words and was amazed. Jesus responded,

"Have faith in God" (vs. 22). In a sense, Jesus was saying, "Why are you surprised?"

Many people look at this story and think, "Why curse the tree if it wasn't the season for figs?" Unlike us, Jesus wasn't having a hissy fit. He wasn't in a bad mood or having a bad hair day (I have those often). He never has those. Jesus also doesn't do anything without purpose. So why did He do this? To model for us the power of faith and the importance of our words as seed. Jesus went on from this experience to teach the disciples how faith speaks.

> *So Jesus answered and said to them, "Have faith in God. For assuredly, I say to you, whoever **says** to this mountain, 'Be removed and be cast into the sea,' and does not doubt in his heart, but believes that those things he **says** will be done, he will have whatever he **says**. **Therefore I** say to you, whatever things you ask when you pray, believe that you receive them, and you will have them."*
>
> Mark 11:22-24

Dear ones, we don't always get what we pray, but we always get what we say. A key to our harvest is learning to say what we pray. Prayer, on its most basic level, is fellowship with God. It also includes petitioning God for the things we desire and need. But prayer is more of a partnership than an intervention. Prayer aligns our heart to God's heart so we can sow faith-filled words for a future harvest. This is a law of the Kingdom. If the abundance of our words sows to one thing, and a moment in our prayer life asks for another, which do you think will prevail?

Early in my walk with the Lord I fell into the trap of believing my prayers could trump my words. I found myself praying one way but saying something else outside my prayer closet. My confessions did not match up. Even when I prayed in faith, I sowed doubt the rest of the day through words of unbelief. Needless to say, I did not see an answer to my prayers.

I know this is a touchy subject. This kind of teaching is often called out as "name it and claim it" or "gab it and grab it." And there have definitely been abuses—on both sides. But regardless of the mockery and unbelief of the gainsayers, or the abuses of the immature, the Word of God is true. Faith speaks. And so does doubt. So instead of saying what we have and sowing seeds of doubt into our future so that those things never change, let's learn to partner with God in faith; believing we can have what we say, not just continuing to say what we have. Let's learn to pray and call those things which are not as though they were.

> *Therefore it is of faith that it might be according to grace, so that the promise might be sure to all the seed, not only to those who are of the law, but also to those who are of the faith of Abraham, who is the father of us all (as it is written, "I have made you a father of many nations") in the presence of Him whom he believed—God, who gives life to the dead and* **calls those things which exist as though they did.**
>
> Romans 4:16-17

Abraham learned how to partner with God in this way. He learned to speak God's words, and he saw those words give life to dead things. He called those things which were not in the natural—his and Sarah's ability to have a child—as though they were. Faith doesn't say what things are. Faith says what is in the spiritual realm and what will be according to God's will and word. Faith doesn't ignore or deny a mountain, but it does speak to it.

Once while Jesus was sailing with His disciples a terrible storm arose. While the disciples panicked, Jesus slept. They woke Jesus begging Him to save them, and Jesus said, *"Why are you fearful, O you of little faith?" Then He arose and rebuked the winds and the sea, and there was a great calm."* (Matt. 8:23-27). Jesus spoke to the storm the same way He spoke to the fig tree. (He spoke to the disciples as well. He corrected them for their lack of faith.) Jesus demonstrated, for us all, how faith speaks.

Jesus would not have corrected the disciples if calming the storm was beyond their authority or ability. He would have comforted them. He would have said something like, "Don't worry boys. I'm here. I'll take care of it. This is too much for you and your faith." But He didn't do that. He modeled how words of faith work like seeds to change our circumstances. That is profound. Jesus expected the disciples to act in the same kind of faith He did. And He expected that they would get the same results.

Before we move on to the next point, let's review what we've learned from this chapter.

Faith Speaks

Faith has been speaking from the beginning. Hebrews 11:3 says, *"By faith we understand that the worlds were framed by the word of God, so that the things which are seen were not made of things which are visible."* Faith is the language of God. By it He spoke the world into existence. He didn't create everything out of nothing. He created everything with faith-filled words so that the seen came out of the unseen. I encourage you to reread Genesis one with this concept in mind. Note the number of times it says, *"And God said..."* and ponder what that means for us who are created in God's image (Gen. 1:26-28). Our words matter. Just like this world was framed by the word of God, our worlds are framed by the words of our mouths. So, choose to speak life over your family and friends. Plant faith-filled words as seed and sow to the harvest you wish to see. Don't allow seeds of doubt and death to take root in your heart and find voice through your words.

While in Bible school I witnessed the destruction of people's ministries in seed form. Their criticisms of the instructors were seeds that surely would produce a harvest later in life. Their self-righteousness in judgment and negative attitudes were not good seed for a desired harvest in their future ministries. Even if someone is wrong, we should treat them with respect and God's kind of love knowing we are sowing to a future harvest.

Speak to the Mountain

When we looked at Mark 11, we saw Jesus tell his disciples to speak to the mountains they were facing. Problems tend to speak loudly; like massive mountains, they are impossible to ignore. But if we dwell on what our mountains are saying, our circumstances will inspire fear when what we need is faith. Instead of repeating whatever words our mountains inspire, let's say what God says. Let's agree with God and sow His Word into the midst of our circumstance. Romans 8 tells us that nothing can separate us from God's love—not trouble or persecution, bad economies or danger, not natural disaster or lack. These things are uncomfortable. They can tend to make us question God's love and care, but Romans 8 tells us how to handle them: *"What then shall we **say** to these things? If God is for us, who can be against us?"* (vs. 31). Notice we are supposed to speak to anything that tries to come between us and God. And what do we say? "God is for me! It doesn't matter what circumstances say. Me and God are a majority, and we win!" Our words may not produce the quick results Jesus saw, but they will bear fruit if we do not give up (Gal. 6:9).

Our Harvest

Remember, not everything in our orbit grew from seeds we have sown. Other people sow seeds, too. Some who haven't read this book, choose to sow bad seeds. Their bad seeds can create a negative harvest around us. Bad things happen to good people. While we reap what we sow, it is also true that we reap where we did not sow, both good and bad. In Matthew 13, Jesus told a parable of a man who sowed a field of wheat. Later that evening, his enemy came and sowed tares in his field. After the grain sprouted, the weeds became evident. But instead of uprooting all that was planted, the man left both the wheat and the tares to grow together. Jesus explained that in the day of judgement, God would separate the tares from the wheat (vs. 24-30, 36-43). Notice that God is the Separator. Instead of worrying about the evil that surrounds us we need to trust the Lord of the Harvest to separate the good and bad in our life. Keep planting good seed with the words of your mouth and watch as your world is reframed by faith.

Say What We Pray

We must partner with God in prayer. Dear ones, we will have what we say. But if we want to move beyond what we've experienced, we need to say what we pray. Like we saw in the Gospel of Mark, *"Therefore I say to you, whatever things you ask when you pray, believe that you receive them, and you will have them"* (11:24). God wills only good in our lives. But He doesn't force that will upon us. He asks us to partner with Him in faith (Heb. 11:6). Too often, we fall into the trap of saying what we have instead of agreeing with God to have what He says we can have. That is not to say we cannot or should not acknowledge problems or negative circumstances in our life. But we need to be intentional about the seeds we are sowing. If all we say is what we have—"I'm always sick. I never have enough money. I'll never get that promotion."—then we'll never experience any other harvest. If we say what God says, and plant those words as seed in our hearts, eventually we will reap a harvest that aligns with His word and will. We cannot pray one way, then say the opposite—whether out loud or in our hearts—for the rest of the day. Our faith seeds need to match the harvest we desire. If we pray God's will be done on earth as it is in heaven, we have to learn to stand on that confession. We do this by reminding ourselves of God's goodness and keeping a heart of thanksgiving and praise. When we pray, we believe we receive, and then we experience harvest. We don't believe we receive when we have. We believe we receive when we pray. In between the believing and receiving, we say what we pray.

Forgive!

To wrap up this chapter, we need to dig deep in God's Word and focus on forgiveness. Mark 11:25 says, *"And whenever you stand praying, if you have anything against anyone, forgive him, that your Father in heaven may also forgive you your trespasses."* That's heavy. But it's something many people miss when thinking about partnering with God in sowing and reaping. Everything God does in our life He does in the context of relationship—relationship with Him and relationship with one another. Our relationship with God is easy. He did all the hard work. But we must continually acknowledge our reliance on that work. We must acknowledge that He is Lord of the Harvest and that He watches over the seed of His Word to perform it (Jer. 1:12). And we need to partner with Him as the Gardener of our hearts to weed out any seeds of doubt or unforgiveness that try to sneak in. Unforgiveness is one of the biggest hinderances to our prayer life. It is also the number one enemy of our harvest. Unforgiveness is a poisonous weed. When allowed to linger in our hearts it chokes out the good seed planted there. To uproot these weeds, we must be quick to forgive (Mark 11:25-26 / Matt. 5).

1 Peter 3:10 says, *"He who would love life and see good days, let him refrain his tongue from evil, and his lips from speaking deceit."* We do not have to be victims of our upbringing or circumstances. We can learn to forgive others so that our faith harvest is not hindered. We can love life and see good days, but it all starts with the seed of our words. Let's partner with God to reframe our future. Let's refrain from evil speaking and choose to speak words of faith. Let's be quick to forgive. Unforgiveness unresolved can morph into a *"root of bitterness,"* causing trouble and spreading defilement (Heb. 12:15). Notice that bitterness is described as a root. All roots come from seeds that "spring up." God has forgiven us of so much; let's be quick to forgive even as Christ has forgiven us. Happy planting!

Chapter 6

Our Promise Land

The Lord your God is giving you, "a land flowing with milk and honey," just as the Lord God of your fathers promised you.

Deuteronomy 27:3b

Much of Israel's prosperity was connected to the land God promised Abraham (Gen. 12:1-3, 15:18/ Ex. 6:8, 13:5). Though we see God's miraculous provision for them in the wilderness, sending manna from heaven, that provision was only supposed to last a few days (Psalm 78:25 / Deut. 1:2). God's original plan was just a few days journey that led to a dreamland of milk and honey. It was Israel's unbelief and rebellion that led to a nightmare of lack in the desert. An eleven-day journey from Horeb to Mount Seir to Kadesh Barnea turned into forty years of a desert experience (Deut. 1:2). However, in His love and mercy God provided for them even in the wilderness they chose. Each day, except Saturday (which was the Sabbath), the Israelites gathered angels' food to eat throughout the day. On Friday, twice as much manna fell to the ground to sustain them through

Saturday (Ex. 16:14-26). As long as the Israelites wandered in the wilderness, the Lord sustained them with manna. And as wonderful as that sounds, don't forget, the Israelites soon despised the Lord's provision (Exodus 16 / Num. 11). They were even willing to return to slavery in Egypt if it meant eating something besides manna!

Miracles Versus Blessings

There is a lesson in that for us. While we serve a God of miracles (and we all could use a miracle from time to time), miracles are not God's best and fullest plan for his people. Miracles were never designed to live on and are simply unsustainable. Miracles require a crisis situation—but who wants to live from crisis to crisis? Living in the blessing of God is a much better option. And by His grace that blessing is available to everyone through seedtime and harvest. Remember, when the Israelites finally entered their Promised Land, the manna ceased (Joshua 5:12). It was no longer needed. They could sow and reap the blessings of God.

As shared previously, everything in first creation came from the ground. All that points to the heart, which is the ground for seed to be sown. Everything was created to reproduce after its own kind by seedtime and harvest. Today, all we need to experience a harvest is to activate the good ground of our heart with the seed of God's Word watered by the Holy Spirit. The desert was not good ground for the Israelites. It was not the "land flowing with milk and honey" God promised Abraham. That's why they needed miraculous provision. The desert was a crisis moment in their lives. God didn't ordain that experience to last forty years. The unbelieving spies, the leaders of Israel, did that when they convinced the people that the inhabitants of Canaan were too powerful for them to overcome (Num. 13-14). That generation would not mix faith with the promise and they perished in the wilderness because of unbelief (Heb. 3:19).

Everything Israel needed was in their Promised Land. When God invited them in to partake of His blessings—homes they did not build, wells they did not dig, orchards and vineyards they did not plant—all they had to do was believe and participate in those blessings through faith (Deut. 6:10-12). Originally, they reaped where they did not sow and then they were to sow and reap from the land. The Kingdom of God is our promised land. It, too, flows with milk and honey. In it is everything we need. Through Christ, God has invited us to partake of His blessings—many of which we did not have to labor for. Others labored and we have entered into the blessing of their labors. He asks us to receive by faith, now partnering with Him through sowing and reaping. This teaching bears repeating:

> *Do not be deceived, God is not mocked; for whatever a man sows, that he will also reap. For he who sows to his flesh will of the flesh reap corruption, but he who* **sows to the Spirit** *will of the Spirit reap everlasting life. And let us not grow weary while doing good, for in due season we shall reap if we do not lose heart.*
>
> Galatians 6:7-9

Work Of Faith

Our only work in this partnership is to mix faith with the seed of God's Word and not lose heart as we await the harvest. According to 1 Thessalonians, this work is a work of faith and a labor of love and patience of hope (1:3). It is not a work of the law or self-effort. It requires more than natural hope or endurance. It requires a trust in the goodness and faithfulness of God, and a hopeful patience in Christ. Sowing seeds and reaping a harvest is not a wage or just recompense from God. It is an immutable law of the Kingdom. It is how we receive from our promise land flowing with milk and honey. Our labor in faith is to enter into His rest (Heb. 4:11). Those who do that have ceased from their own works, not good works of faith (Heb. 4:10).

When the miracle of manna ceased for Israel, the natural law of seedtime and harvest that had been suspended for forty years was reinitiated. They had to mix faith with their sowing of seeds. Remember, these were the children of those who had left Egypt and children born in the desert. Many had never experienced the labor or hope associated with planting a crop. They had also not experienced the prosperity that came with its harvest. Even those who labored in Egypt had to give most of what they grew to Pharoah. This first experience required that they labor by faith to see prosperity. It wasn't faith alone, and it wasn't labor alone that made the Israelites prosper. Faith alone is representative of the manna they received from heaven. It sustained them, but it did not prosper them in the wilderness. Labor alone is representative of their time in Egypt. For 430 years Israel labored under Pharoah, but they did not prosper. The Israelites needed both faith and labor—in their own land—to prosper and experience God's blessings.

We need both too. Labor in a foreign land, which is anything outside God's Kingdom and will for our lives, will not prosper us. Unbelief in God's promises is not a recipe for prosperity as well. That does not mean work is not important. There is value in all work. But to experience true prosperity, that work must be done in faith and connected to our land (God's Kingdom).

Giants To Conquer

The parallels don't stop there. Just as Israel faced giants in the land that had to be driven out, we too will face giants in our promised land. Most of them will be giants of our own making—

patterns of behavior, prior ways of thinking, strongholds of fear. To overcome these giants and drive them out, we have to remember that we are qualified to share in these blessings because we have been delivered from the power of darkness and translated us into the Kingdom of God (Col. 1:12-13). We are no longer slaves in Egypt. Nor are we locked into a wilderness of rebellion and disobedience. As residents of His Kingdom, our vocations are connected to that Kingdom. Our careers are sacred not secular. Our work, *all* our work, is now done as unto the Lord (Col. 3:17, 23). In our promised land, my calling as a minister is no more sacred than yours as a teacher, mechanic, or doctor. All honest work is vital to the furthering of God's Kingdom. People in a "secular" vocation have influence with people I never will meet in the church environment. They have a witness for Christ in places I cannot go. And all of us can prosper in our work as long as we labor by faith. All the giants in our promise land are as grasshoppers in our sight NOT vice versa. We are well able to possess our land in Christ.

God's Image

You may not realize this, but work is part of the image of God in man. God worked in creation. He worked for six days, and on the seventh, rested (Gen. 2:2). Jesus came and did the "works" of the Father (John 9:4, 10:32, 37-38). And so, man also works. To not work, when we are capable of work, is to become less than human. Government handouts are not the path to prosperity. There is no prosperity for you on the welfare of Egypt. It isn't even charity as some would have you believe. Charity is voluntary. It comes from a heart of love. Taking from one group to give to another is not charity. It is evil. It locks people into dependency and distorts the image of God expressed in mankind. Governments cannot create wealth; they can only squander it and abuse it. Depending on the government will never allow you to move beyond survival. Look at the animals. Animals don't work, except under the control of man. Everything they do is for survival. Humans build houses, businesses, hospitals and civilizations. We create art and music which reflect God's image in man. Someone might say, "What about the beavers? They work. They build dams." But beavers do that for survival, and they've done so for thousands of years. They aren't creating, improving, and expanding order. That's the unique expression of God's image in man. Beavers don't have new and improved dams every ten years. (Ever seen a high-rise beaver condo?)

Our work is part of our worship to God (Eph. 6:6/ Col. 3:17, 22-23). We worship God by expressing His image in the Earth. We serve Him by serving others. That's the difference between laboring as slaves in Egypt and laboring in the Kingdom, even if our occupations do not change after we are saved. Our work now has a Kingdom focus. It is no longer focused on greed and selfish ambition. Now we work to provide for our families and give to those in need. We work to serve our communities and our fellow man. We build hospitals and care for the sick because of God's image of compassion in us.

If scripture sees our giving as an act of worship, then our work to be able to give is also an act of worship. Ephesians 4:28 says, *"Let him who stole steal no longer, but rather let him* **labor, working** *with his hands what is good, that he may have something to give him that has need."* We are commanded to work. The fourth commandment says, *"Remember the Sabbath day, to keep it holy"* (Ex. 20:8). But there's no reason for a sabbath if we don't work. That's why the commandment of rest comes out of a commandment to work: *"Six days you shall* **labor** *and do all your* **work**, *but the seventh day is the Sabbath of the Lord your God. In it you shall do no work"* (Ex. 20:9-10a). So, work hard. Trust God to supernaturally prosper you as you work, and do not forget to honor Him by observing a day of rest—your body needs it, and your mind and spirit do, too. The New Testament reiterates this command when Paul said that a man who doesn't work shouldn't eat (2 Thess. 3:8-10). "That sure sounds harsh!" Not if you understand that work is part of God's image in man and an expression of our worship of God. Not working damages God's image in us and limits our positive impact on our communities.

Our work has purpose in the Kingdom of God, for both men and women. In Proverbs 31 the virtuous woman provides for her family with real estate, trade, physical labor, and farming. She gives to the needy. She speaks with wisdom and kindness. And verse 31 says, *"Give her the fruit of her hands, and let her own works praise her in the gates."* The fruit of our hands, when blessed by God, leads to our prosperity. The fruit of our lips changes the course of our lives. There is no need to covet other's prosperity, because now we can sow to our own. Believe God's Word and learn to mix faith with the labor of your hands. Don't worry about putting a number on success. Partner with God and you will see your life begin to change. That's the kind of prosperity God offers a prosperity that covers more than income—and He adds no sorrow with it (Prov. 10:22).

God told Israel (and consequently, us), "When you enter the land and begin to prosper, do not forget Me. Do not forget how you came to be where you are. Remember the source of your prosperity and remember why it was given to you—to establish My covenant" (Deut. 6:10-12; 8:17-18 paraphrased). Doing things God's way leads to blessing. Deuteronomy 28:1-2 says:

> *Now it shall come to pass, if you diligently obey the voice of the Lord your God, to observe carefully all His commandments which I command you today, that the Lord your God will set you high above all nations of the*

earth. And all these blessings shall come upon you and overtake you, because you obey the voice of the Lord your God:

Our faith in Jesus and His obedience to the Father gives us access to all these blessings and deliverance from all the curses (Gal. 3:13-14). Let's continue in Deuteronomy 28 to see what those blessing are in Christ:

> *Blessed shall you be in the city, and blessed shall you be in the country. Blessed shall be the fruit of your body,* **the produce of your ground** *and the increase of your herds, the increase of your cattle and the offspring of your flocks. Blessed shall be your basket and your kneading bowl. Blessed shall you be when you come in, and blessed shall you be when you go out. The Lord will cause your enemies who rise against you to be defeated before your face; they shall come out against you one way and flee before you seven ways. The Lord will command the blessing on you in your* **storehouses** *and in all to which you* **set your hand**, *and He will* **bless you in the land** *which the Lord your God is giving you.* (vs. 3-8)

How many people have felt they had to leave the small town where they grew up to make a living in the city? That's not what God says. God blesses you wherever you are. In your promised land, your kids are blessed. Your work is blessed. You are blessed whether you come in or go out because your blessing is connected to your faith in God. It's not about your circumstances. Notice that the Lord commanded a blessing on your storehouses and all you set your hand to in the *land* He has given you.

Storehouses

Our prosperity is tied to our promised land, the Kingdom of God. There, God blesses whatever we put our hands to. Again, that has nothing to do with the *type* of work you do. It has everything to do with trusting God as your source. Remember it is He who gives you the power to get wealth (Deut. 8:18). Be a good steward of what you are given and keep His Kingdom first (Matt. 25:14-28, 6:33/ 1 Peter 4:10). That doesn't mean you have to constantly be at church. Attending church is part of keeping His Kingdom first, but not all. We should be seeking God's Kingdom and apply Kingdom principles in our careers, our relationships, our health, our families, and every other aspect of our lives. As we do these things, God blesses our storehouses, plural. The church is just one of those storehouses (Mal. 3:10). Having other storehouses is part of good stewardship. (If we're going to trust God to bless our seed, we need to have places to put it!) Your 401k can be a storehouse. Land can be a storehouse. Our businesses can be storehouses, too. They bless our communities by offering people jobs and putting food on people's tables. They allow us to be producers and givers, not just takers. God blesses faith, faithfulness, and stewardship: *"He who is faithful in what is least is faithful also in much; and he who is unjust in what is least is unjust also in much"* (Luke 16:10). Our stewardship of our harvest on seeds sown is important. Handling the prosperity that comes with our harvest is as important as the sowing of our seeds. Jesus ties our faithfulness with natural things to our connection to the true riches which is love for people (Luke 16:11-13).

Rest

Part of doing things God's way is taking time to rest. When Israel sowed in the Promised Land, they were supposed to rest the land every seventh day and every seventh year. During that year they were not to work the land at all. They weren't even supposed to harvest what grew wild in their fields. It sounds crazy, but in the sixth year God blessed their trust and obedience and the people harvested double. Their harvests were so large, they had enough to survive the year the land rested and plant for the following. This same thing happened on a larger scale during the Year of Jubilee. The year of Jubilee was a sabbath of sabbaths (seven years of seven totaling 49 years). Jubilee was celebrated during the fiftieth year and the land had to rest for two years (49-50) then sowing took place in the third year. In the forty-eighth year they reaped a three-fold harvest to sustain them until they planted again. God blessed their seed sown to provide for them those three years. (Lev 25)

Another aspect of doing things God's way is learning to look at your work as an avenue to help those in need. Jobs provide us with seed to sow. Though a job is never the source of our prosperity, God uses it to provide us with seed. He then works with our seed and blesses the ground where we sow to produce a harvest so we can give. So, in all my labor, I am truly laboring to give. It is in this sowing and reaping and giving (sowing again) that God is able to bring true prosperity to our lives. The harvest from my sown seed fills the storehouses in my land, and my giving lays up treasures for me in heaven (Matthew 6:19-21). What a blessing!

Proverbs 3:9-10 says, *"Honor the Lord with your possessions, and with the firstfruits of all your increase; so your **barns** will be filled with plenty, and your **vats** will overflow with new wine."* First fruits refers to the tithe throughout scripture. Notice that honoring God with giving on your increase causes your barns (plural) and vats (plural) to be filled and overflow. God blesses our stewardship with plenty to increase our giving thus laying up treasures in heaven.

Don't get trapped into thinking, "I need to work more." Or "I need a higher paying job." That's the way you thought before God translated you into His Kingdom. Your job is not the source of your prosperity. God is your source. True prosperity realizes, the more money I make, the more seeds I have to sow. 2 Corinthians nine explains this highest form of prosperity—giving. In it, Paul says, *"But this I say: he who sows sparingly will also reap sparingly, and he who sows bountifully will also reap bountifully. So let each one give as he purposes in his heart, not grudgingly or of necessity; for God loves a cheerful giver. And God is able to make all grace abound toward you, that you, always having all sufficiency in all things, may have an* **abundance for every good work**" (vs. 6-8). God prospers us so we can have enough to give to every good work. And verse ten says, *"Now may He who supplies seed to the sower, and bread for food, supply and multiply the seed you have sown and increase the fruits of your righteousness."* It's hard not to get excited about that! Sowing increases the fruits of our righteousness. Our giving is not just natural. It is spiritual and supernatural.

Look at it again. *Now may He who supplies...* If you thought your boss supplied, now you know why you've been feeling stuck. God supplies. He is our source. He is the One who gives us the strength and ability to work. He gives us the wisdom to build businesses, the creativity to solve problems. He provides seed to the sower and bread for food. The Lord of the Harvest ensures to supply and multiply the seeds you have sown and increase the fruits of your righteousness. That's incredible. God blesses the works of our hands. He increases our testimony as a showpiece of His goodness, so the world can see how He treats His kids.

The fruit of our righteousness is our giving to others in need. It could include giving to the poor or other charity groups doing great things. Maybe giving into missions or other ministries that are preaching the gospel. Even in our storehouses our seed sown is multiplying in order to bless us and make us a blessing in the future. Sowing bountifully includes many storehouses for a plentiful harvest. This whole time we are laying up treasures in heaven seeing lives changed for God's glory and kingdom. Our giving to righteous works increases the fruit of righteousness. I have fruit from seeds sown for this life and fruit laid up in heaven for eternity.

So, in wrapping up this chapter, the Kingdom is our promised land. It is our God-given place of work and blessing. All our work is a work of faith, labor of love, and patience of hope in our harvest (1 Thess. 1:3). While there are giants in the Kingdom to be driven out, it is a good fight, a fight of faith from a position of victory in Christ, not a fight for victory (1 Tim. 6:12). Our handling of natural things is spiritual and our faithfulness in the little (sowing seeds) will make us ruler of much (a bountiful harvest). Welcome to a promised land flowing with milk and honey.

Chapter 7

Parable of the Sower

The kingdom of God is as if a man should scatter seed on the ground.

Mark 4:26

The truths shared in the Parable of the Sower are extensive. But each of those truths begins and ends with our willingness to hear. "Listen!" Jesus says before continuing to teach in Mark chapter four: *"Behold, a sower went out to sow…"* (Mark 4:3). The seed, He said, fell in a variety of places and did not produce or produced based on the condition of the ground. Then, as Jesus finished sharing this story He tells His hearers, *"He who has ears to hear, **let him hear!**"* (vs. 9). We must choose to hear or we won't. Choose to listen, focus, and then hear. This admonition is repeated to the churches in the book of Revelation (Rev. 2:7 / 2:11 / 2:17 / 2:29 / 3:6 / 3:13 / 3:22). To hear is to understand.

We have to choose to hear. If we don't, we will miss the things God is saying. Even in the natural world, our minds were not created to track every piece of stimuli that enters it. In order to focus we have to be able to tune some things out. Most people do this subconsciously. They don't have to think about it. When in a room with white noise, we stop hearing things like the air conditioner or background music. In restaurants we don't hear other table's conversations unless we choose to eavesdrop. This same thing happens in our spiritual life. We have to choose to hear God or we won't. We all have an ear to hear but must develop a listening and obedient ear.

Let's look at the Parable of the Sower and choose to hear what the Lord is saying. Jesus shared this parable while teaching the multitudes near Galilee. It goes like this:

> **"Listen!** *Behold, a sower went out to sow. And it happened, as he sowed, that some seed fell by the wayside; and the birds of the air came and devoured it. Some fell on stony ground, where it did not have much earth; and immediately it sprang up because it had no depth of earth. But when the sun was up it was scorched, and because it had no root it withered away. And some seed fell among thorns; and the thorns grew up and choked it, and it yielded no crop. But other seed fell on good ground and yielded a crop that sprang up, increased and produced: some thirtyfold, some sixty, and some a hundred." And He said to them, "He who has ears to hear,* **let him hear!**"*

Mark 4:3-9

Later, while Jesus was alone with the disciples, He explained the meaning of the parable. He told them that understanding this parable was key to understanding all parables. Mark 4:13 says, *"Do you not understand this parable? How then will you understand all the parables?"* That's how important this mystery of God's Kingdom is. In case you're not familiar with this terminology, a parable is an earthly story with a heavenly meaning. Jesus used parables throughout His ministry to express the mysteries of the Kingdom. Just as His disciples sought the spiritual understanding of these stories, we too must "ask, seek, and knock" to uncover the treasures of the Kingdom that have been hidden for our benefit (Matt. 7:7-8/ Psalm 25:14). Asking, seeking, and knocking helps us develop a healthy relationship with the Lord. It is also a key to progressive change in our lives.

The Sower

Jesus told His disciples that *the Sower sowed the Word* (Mark 4:14). Anyone who shares God's Word, in love, is a Sower (Eph. 4:15). Sowing or sharing God's Word is the only way people can have faith to be saved or changed (Rom. 10:17). So, we must cast the precious seed of the Kingdom everywhere we go. Speaking the truth in love is the work of a Sower.

Many believers think that the Kingdom of God is heaven. But the Kingdom is everywhere Jesus, the King of the Kingdom, reigns. As we learn to partner with God and yield to His Lordship and leadership, that Kingdom begins to permeate every aspect of our lives—our families, our careers, our finances, our health, everything. This is our promised land. In one parable, Jesus said the Kingdom was *"like leaven, which a woman took and **hid** in three measures of meal till it was all leavened"* (Matt. 13:33). God's Kingdom is hidden in our hearts, but in time will leaven our souls, bodies, and lives. Remember, when Israel entered their Promised Land, they were tasked with driving out the giants and other inhabitants of the land. There are no giants in heaven. There are no unlawful inhabitants. So, heaven, as wonderful as it will be, is not our promised land. Our land is here, on earth. It is in whatever sphere God calls us to under the authority of Jesus. The Kingdom is on the inside of every believer in Jesus (Col. 1:13). Sharing the good news of the Kingdom and Jesus as Lord makes us all Sowers.

The Seed

The seed, Jesus said, is God's Word (Mark 4:14). Like all seeds, God's Word is full of life. His life lives in every promise—both written and spoken—and when planted as seed, it will reproduce after its own kind. As previously mentioned, Mary experienced this truth when she believed the word Gabriel brought and conceived the Christ. We also experience this truth when we are born again. 1 Peter 1:23 says we are born again of the incorruptible seed of God's Word. When we believe the Word concerning Jesus, that seed reproduces after its own kind. It makes us new (Ez. 36:25-27/ Rom. 6:3-4/ 2 Cor. 5:17). Every seed of God's Word has this power within it. It only needs to be mixed with faith and planted in the womb of our heart (Heb. 4:2). Our hearts are the good ground ready for the seed of God's Word. Given time and the watering of the Holy Spirit, that seed will produce a harvest. It will fulfill itself (Jer. 1:12). God's Word is both seed for our future and food for our present (Is. 55:11/ 1 Peter 2:2).

The Ground

Jesus likened the ground of the parable to men's hearts. He said there were four types of ground (which we will unpack in more detail in just a bit) that receive the Word in various ways. Some hearts are hard and stony. The seed sown on this type of ground is quickly lost. Other hearts receive the Word, but because the ground is not ready for seed—it may be shallow or full of weeds—it never bears fruit. Only one type of heart was considered "good ground" and it is able to produce a harvest off the seed of God's Word.

Lest you think there's no hope for you, remember God took away our old, stony heart at the new birth. God promised Ezekiel,

*"And I will give you a new heart, and I will put a new spirit in you. I will take out your **stony, stubborn heart** and give you a tender, responsive heart. And I will put my Spirit in you so that you will follow my decrees and be careful to obey my regulations"* (Ez. 36:26-27, NLT). With this soft, pliable heart we are able to receive His Word into good ground. But we must be careful to guard our hearts from weeds. Our hearts are like fertile ground. They were not created to discriminate against seed. They will bring forth fruit from any seed sown into it. If we want to see a particular type of harvest, we must be seed discriminators before those seeds are sown. Otherwise, if we sow lust, we will reap adultery. If we sow hate, we will reap murder. But if we sow God's Word, we will reap its life and blessings.

The Enemy of the Harvest

Jesus also taught that certain elements of this world wage war against the seed sown in our hearts. In Mark 4, He outlines the tactics Satan uses to make us barren in God's Kingdom. Distraction, persecutions, offense, worry, lust, and misplaced trust in riches are seeds that fight for space in our hearts. Like weeds, they steal resources from the ground and war against the seed of God's Word. But even in these things Jesus partners with us as the Gardener of our hearts. As we repent, He helps us weed out those things that cause us to be unproductive so we can reap a harvest off God's Word instead and bear much fruit.

Remember, the Kingdom of God rotates around the principle of seedtime and harvest. Seed is how God fulfills His promises. Immediately after Adam and Eve sinned, God promised a redeemer. He said that redeemer would come as the seed of the woman to crush the serpent's head. Speaking to the serpent, God said: *"And I will put enmity between you and the woman, and between your seed and **her Seed**; He shall bruise your head, and you shall bruise His* *heel"* (Gen. 3:15). Not only is this the first Messianic prophecy in scripture, it also foretells the virgin birth. Women do not have seed, men do. Through this virgin birth would come the promised seed (Jesus) and He would crush Satan's head (Gal. 3:16). No wonder Satan fights against seed (Rev. 12:17)! Our salvation came from a promised Seed, and now the enemy's only hope of prevailing against the Church is barrenness. Satan knows that if the seed of God's Word takes root in our hearts, we will bear fruit and glorify God (John 15:8). When we learn to abide in the Word, to let that seed multiply and transform our lives, we will overcome the schemes of the enemy and be able to recover others from his snares as well. Let's look at the four types of ground Jesus mentioned in Mark four and see how the condition of our hearts can affect the seed of God's Word.

The Wayside

As Jesus explained the parable to His disciples, He said, *"And these are the ones by the wayside where the word is sown. When they hear, Satan comes immediately and takes away the word that was sown in their hearts"* (Mark 4:15). The "wayside" was a pathway around a farmer's field. It was exposed to a lot of foot traffic, so the ground was hard and packed. In the parable, when any seed fell on this path, birds immediately came to eat it. The seed never took root, so there was no fruit.

Jesus said the birds represented Satan. He is the enemy who comes immediately to steal the Word. Mark doesn't explain how Satan does this, but Matthew does in his telling of this parable. Matthew says, *"When anyone hears the word of the kingdom, and **does not understand it**, then the wicked one comes and snatches away what was sown in his heart. This is he who received seed by the wayside"* (Matt. 13:19). Hard hearts are easy targets for Satan's schemes. A hard heart does not understand the Word. Anyone who chooses to hear (understand) can and will. The lack of understanding God's Word or will is demonic. It is a spiritual battle to understand, not a natural one. It's not an intellectual problem or a mental deficiency, but rather an attitude of the heart that allows Satan to steal God's Word. By keeping a sensitive and open heart to God, we can understand God's Word and will for our lives. It is only with hard hearts that Satan is able to steal the seed.

An example of this type of hardened heart comes from the story of the Exodus. When Moses approached Pharaoh demanding the Israelites release, scripture says Pharoah hardened his heart to the point that God gave him what he desired—a hard heart (Ex. 9:12). God used Pharoah as a forever example of a hard heart. Pharoah refused to listen to Moses' pleas—even in the midst of severe judgement—and actually made life harder for the Israelites and his people, the Egyptians. His hard heart blinded him to the suffering his own people endured during the ten plagues, ending with the tenth one being the loss of every firstborn throughout the land. It led to his foolish decision to pursue God's people through the Red Sea. In case you don't know the story, God parted the sea for His people to leave Egypt. They crossed on dry ground, but Pharoah and his entire army were drowned (Ex. 15:4-5).

No sane person, after witnessing the might of God's judgement during the ten plagues, would have pursued the Israelites into the desert. (Pharaoh wouldn't have either had he not been consumed with pride and a hard heart.) No one would have pushed their armies into the depths of the sea with a wall of water hemming them in on either side. But Pharaoh's hardness of heart blinded him. It stole his understanding and practical common sense. Hebrews says that sin does the same thing. It hardens the heart through deceitfulness (Heb. 3:8, 13). That is why we need to repent quickly when we fail. Repentance keeps our hearts soft and sensitive to God's Word. It allows us to receive the Word and get revelation from it. Psalm 119:130 says, *"The entrance of Your words gives **light**; it gives **understanding** to the simple."* When our hearts are pure it is easy to hear and see God. Matthew 5:8 instructs us, *"Blessed are the pure in heart, for they shall see God."* Pure here means single-minded, not mixed or diluted. It's like 100% pure orange juice, not mixed with other flavors or additives. This phrase "pure in heart" does not mean perfectly holy, but rather single in devotion. A single or simple-minded heart understands God's Word and will. This is why we see such foolishness and insanity in our world today, hard hearts! Revelation of God's Word defeats Satan. It renews our minds and transforms our lives (Rom. 12:2).

Our lack of understanding of God's ways and kingdom is not a reflection of our IQ. It is spiritual, not natural, and in some cases demonic. Jesus said that we do not understand the Word because Satan "snatches it away." Anyone can understand God's Word and ways when they choose to hear and have a pure heart.

Stony Ground

Jesus continued His explanation of the parable by saying, *"These likewise are the ones sown on stony ground who, when they hear the word, immediately receive it with gladness; and they have no **root** in themselves, and so endure only for a time. Afterward, when tribulation or persecution arises for the word's sake, immediately they stumble"* (Mark 4:16-17). In this ground, the Word doesn't really take root. Satan pulls the seed up through hardships before it takes deep root. People who have not made an effort to cultivate the soil of their hearts—whether they are new believers trying to survive outside a community of faith or immature Christians who run from discipleship—sprout seeds with shallow root systems. They may receive God's Word joyfully, but as soon as persecution or trials come that challenge God's Word they stumble. The King James Version of Mark 4:17 says that these hearts "are offended." Offense, whether at God or other believers, is another way Satan steals the Word from our hearts. Every time we are offended, we abort the process of seedtime and harvest. We forfeit the seed's power to transform our lives and drink a deadly poison. Boy, that should explain a lot.

Paul said, in Acts 24:16, that he always strived *"to have a conscience without offense toward God and men."* That means he had to work at it; you and I will, too. But we can overcome this scheme of the enemy by understanding God's true nature and learning to forgive others. Psalm 119 reminds us, *"Great peace have they which love thy law: and nothing shall offend them"* (vs. 165, KJV). If you think Satan may be causing barrenness in your life over offense, I encourage you to get my book, *Erasing Offense*. In it, I go into great detail about this scheme and explain how we can overcome it to lead fruitful lives.

For now, it is important to know unresolved offense leads to unforgiveness which then becomes a root of bitterness. Hebrews 12:15 says, *"looking carefully lest anyone fall short of the grace of God; lest any **root of bitterness** springing up cause **trouble**, and by this many become **defiled**."* Notice that bitterness is referred to as a "root." Jesus taught that the process of our harvest is, *"...first the blade, then the ear, after that the full corn in the ear"* (Mark 4:28, KJV). The negative harvest of bitterness starts with a blade of offense, then unforgiveness becomes the ear and bitterness the full corn in the ear. Learn to not "take offense" and be quick to forgive. So many good Christian people become needless casualties of offense. They not only become barren in fruit-bearing, but they also become bitter causing them to be defiled. This is so senseless and unnecessary.

Thorny Ground

About the seed sown among thorns Jesus said, *"they are the ones who hear the word, and the cares of this world, the deceitfulness of riches, and the desires for other things entering in* **choke** *the word, and it becomes unfruitful"* (Mark 4:18-19). In the natural world, weedy, thorny ground competes with seed for sunlight, moisture, and nutrients within the soil. Since these plants are typically well established, new seeds simply cannot survive. In the spiritual realm, the seed of God's Word (though incredibly powerful) is often choked out by established thought patterns and behaviors that lead us away from relationship with the Lord. Thoughts are seeds and like weeds must be displaced and replaced with God's thoughts. God's Word reveals His thoughts and provides us with nothing but good precious seed (Is. 55:8-11).

If you've worked with people as long as I have, this idea explains a lot of the barrenness we see in the Church. Christians are so busy trying to survive the world they forget they are no longer part of it. Toward the end of Jesus' ministry on Earth, He prayed for those who would believe on Him:

> *I have given them Your word; and the world has hated them because* ***they are not of the world****, just as I am not of the world. I do not pray that You should take them out of the world, but that You should keep them from the evil one.* ***They are not of the world****, just as I am not of the world. Sanctify them by Your truth. Your word is truth. As You sent Me into the world, I also have sent them into the world.*
>
> John 17:14-18

As followers of Jesus, we are no longer part of this world. We've been translated into God's Kingdom. And though we do have to live in this world, we are kept from the evil one—we are set apart and made holy—by God's Word. (Sanctify means "to set apart.") When we allow the cares of this world, the deceitfulness of riches, and the lust of other things into our hearts we become unfruitful. These things choke out the Word. Thankfully, Jesus, the Gardener of our hearts, is ready to help us uproot these thorns and replant the good seed of God's Word. Let's look at how to deal with these thorns that threaten our harvest.

Cares of this World

The cares of this world are all the things that distract us from faith in God. They influence us to worry about or fear the future. 1 Peter 5:7 says we combat this by casting our care on the Lord. Peter goes on to say, *"Be sober, be vigilant; because your adversary the devil walks about like a roaring lion, seeking whom he may devour. Resist him, steadfast in the faith"* (vs. 8-9a). The enemy of our souls seeks to devour our seed through worry and care, which are just symptoms of fear. We resist him by faith. But notice how this faith operates—with a sober mind. You may not know this, but faith is connected to our thoughts.

A sober mind is one free from the toxic lies and ways of the world. Many people have a heart drunken with worry, anxiety, and fear. They are intoxicated with the WOKE philosophies of men and are in a drunken stupor on the world's thinking. Jesus spoke of this condition of men's hearts in the last days: *"And take heed to yourselves, lest at any time your hearts be overcharged with surfeiting, and **drunkenness**, and cares of this life…"* (Luke 21:34 KJV). Notice that the heart can be overcharged with drunkenness and cares. A drunken heart filled with cares overcharges (overloads) the heart leading to fruitlessness. A sober mind (heart) is focused on God's goodness and faithfulness in all things. The prophet Isaiah says it like this: *"You will keep him in perfect peace, whose **mind** is stayed on

You, because he trusts in You. Trust the Lord forever, for in YAH, the Lord, is everlasting strength."

Many misguided Christians believe they are walking and living by faith, but their minds are not on the Lord. They are meditating on problems (worry) rather than on God's promises and faithfulness. We cannot separate our thought life from our faith walk: *"For to be carnally minded is death, but to be spiritually minded is life and peace"* (Rom. 8:6).

Notice how the choice of thoughts affects the quality of life. We must displace old worldly thoughts and replace them with God's thoughts, *"For as [a man] thinks in his heart, so is he"* (Prov. 23:7a).

Thoughts are seeds. And as we've already seen, our dominate thoughts will affect our lives. Worry comes from meditating on lies. When we worry, our imagination is seeing (or having faith in) a worst-case scenario. Jesus said, *"Which of you by worrying can add one cubit to his stature?"* (Matt. 6:27). Worry accomplishes nothing of eternal value. But to replace those thoughts with faith thoughts requires a change of mind. It requires humility—a recognition that our way is not the best way (Is. 55:8). We assault the thorn of care by meditating on God's Word.

The Deceit of Riches

The deceitfulness of riches is another thorn that chokes out God's Word. Riches are not evil. However, deceit often comes with those riches, and that is deadly. I Timothy 6:10 reads, *"The **love** of money is the root of all evil: which while some coveted after, they have erred from the faith, and pierced themselves through with many sorrows"* (KJV). Wow. This verse has a lot to say. First, notice that the *love* of money, not money itself, is the root of all evil. Money is amoral. It's just a tool, a way of functioning in society. It is an excellent servant, but it makes a terrible master. The love of money breeds deceit that can lead us away from God—and both the rich and poor fall into its trap. What is this deceit? The idea that money can solve all our problems. Or that if we just had a little more, we could be happy or more generous. But Jesus said giving was an issue of the heart, not an issue of the wallet or income bracket (Luke 16:10, 21:3-4).

The cure for this thorn is thankfulness and generosity (1 Cor. 9:6-10). Matthew six says, *"But lay up for yourselves treasures in heaven, where neither moth nor rust destroys and where thieves do not break in and steal. For where your treasure is, there your heart will be also"* (vs. 20-21). The heart always follows the treasure and our treasures will follow our hearts. Show me the money and I'll show you the heart. When we give cheerfully, as 2 Corinthians commands, we lay mammon (the love of money) at the feet of Jesus (Matt. 6:24). Thankfulness for what we have keeps us in faith and away from any deceit. Thankfulness is the voice of faith.

Lust of Things

The lust of other things is a reference to covetousness. Covetousness is idolatry (Col. 3:5). When we covet, we open the door for Satan to steal the Word. We invite him in to destroy our lives and relationships (1 Cor. 10:19-20; John 10:10). Covetousness is toxic. People covet power. They covet man's approval, another's spouse, another's job, even another's ministry gift. And many in the church do not recognize it. They have become so immersed in the darkness of the world they don't recognize the darkening of their own hearts (2 Cor. 10:12). In Romans chapter one, Paul describes the process of the hardening of the heart. It begins with a choice to not recognize or glorify God as God, then progresses to being unthankful. Idolatry is not far behind, and soon the lust of the flesh drives people into all kinds of other evils.

Worship is the way to weed out this thorn. Developing a heart that hungers for God helps us submit to His Word. It reminds us of who God is, our Source, and that He wills nothing but good for us. This drives us to thanksgiving, no matter what circumstances we face, and helps us guard our hearts in prayer (1 Thes. 5:18). God deserves our worship of Him and Him alone. He is a jealous God. His very name is Jealous (Ex. 34:14).

Good Ground

Finally, Jesus explains the good ground of His parable. This ground is the heart that hears the Word, accepts it, and bears much fruit—some 30, 60, or 100 times what was sown (Mark 4:20). Matthew says this ground belongs to the one who hears and understands the Word (13:23).

The first ground that was fruitless has no understanding. The good ground bore fruit because of understanding. The thirty, sixty, hundredfold yield is connected to the level of our understanding. All understanding (revelation) is the ceiling of our present fruitfulness but the floor to our future. Each revelation of God is a building block to the house of wisdom and a life of fruit bearing.

Throughout my years of ministry, I've been amazed to see how many professed Christians reject God's Word. Culture has deceived them, and they have become "dull of hearing" (Heb. 5:11). They need to be retaught the simple truths of the Kingdom (Heb. 5:12).

Dear ones, you are either progressing or digressing in your walk with the Lord. No one can coast uphill! When we choose to hear (and keep hearing) God's Word, we grow (Rom. 10:17).

When we allow ourselves to become dull of hearing, we quit bearing fruit. We go backwards.

When combating the philosophies of man, we have to let God be true and every man a liar (Rom. 3:4). We have to choose which seeds we will receive. Many people hear God's Word but believe what is said on the six o'clock news over the truth of God's Word. They read God's thoughts (His word), then run after man's opinion. In order to bear fruit, we have to accept God's Word as final authority—even if it contradicts "so-called science" or flies in the face of political correctness or woke nonsense. Much of science today has been hijacked by political agendas and is corrupted because of it. It is more science fiction than pure science. We have to understand that God's Word is true (Psalm 19:7-11). It created all things and continues to sustain all things by its power (John 1:1-3 / Heb. 1:3).

Remember, the ground by the wayside could not bear fruit because its hearers did not understand the Word that was sown. But good ground hears, receives, and understands the Word. It bears fruit—some 30, 60, or 100 times what was sown. The difference in harvest is determined by how well we guard and garden our hearts. How well do we hear? Are we guarding our hearts against offense? Are we quick to forgive? How do we receive the Word? Do we accept God's Word as final authority, or do we waiver between what it says and what the world says? Are we diligently weeding out distractions so we can understand what is being said? When we don't understand, do we ask clarifying questions, or do we question God? We all have the potential to bear a hundredfold return. But we cannot ignore the condition of our hearts, the ground.

Chapter 8

Reaping Where We Do Not Sow

For in this the saying is true: 'One sows and another reaps.'

John 4:37

I have mentioned this saying of Jesus several times, but it bears repeating. While we certainly reap what we sow, we do not always reap what we personally sowed to (good or bad). It sounds like a paradox, but if we do not understand this mystery we could be condemned or lifted up in pride over circumstances beyond our control. Worse yet, we might condemn (or idolize) others when those things happen in their lives. We have all experienced good and bad things to which we did not sow. That is part of the sufferings of living in a fallen world (bad things) and the blessings of God's Kingdom (good things).

Jesus declares that one sows but another reaps, meaning there is a truth of reaping where we did not sow. When Jesus said *"…in this the saying is true; one sows and another reaps,"* what did He mean? In other words, this truth had already been revealed in the Old Testament. Reaping where we do not sow was not a new revelation or just a New Testament truth. The story of Job offers an important example for us when it comes to reaping where we did not sow.

Look at Job

Job was a man of integrity who worshiped the Lord and shunned evil. The Bible calls him "blameless" and "upright" (Job 1:1). Again in Job 1:8 God said His servant Job was unlike any other person on earth, a perfect man who feared God and was without evil. God repeats this remarkable statement once again in Chapter 2 verse 3. Three times God said Job was perfect, upright, and fled evil, yet when sorrow and tribulation came to Job, his friends insisted he had sinned or "sowed bad seeds" to reap the trouble he was experiencing. They knew nothing of the mystery of reaping where we do not sow. While Job was a sinner by nature because of being sold out to sin and Satan by Adam, what sin could he have committed worthy of such a horrific harvest? God said Job was blameless, not sinless. Job was faithful to offer sacrifices, and God received the offerings which made his servant blameless before Him. In the course of time, Satan attacked Job and stole everything from him—his wealth, his health, his servants, even his family (all ten children were killed in one day). The only thing Satan left to "comfort" Job during these attacks was Job's wife and misguided friends. (If you know the story, neither were very encouraging.) Job's wife told him to *"curse God and die"* (Job 2:9). His friends condemned him without cause (Job 32:3). They thought he must have sinned, and it must have been a terrible sin, to bring about such a bad harvest (Job 4:7, 8:6, 11:6, 22:4-5). God was not pleased with their assumption (Job 42:7). He even testified of Job's integrity so that we would not fall into the same trap as his friends (Job 1:1, 1:8, 2:3, three witnesses). Yet I still hear people condemn Job or stretch the scriptures to find a "reason" for his suffering—either in Job's heart or God's. What are we missing? Do we not believe Jesus' words? Is it not possible for Job to have reaped where he did not sow? Why would God testify to how perfect and upright he was...if he wasn't?

God's heart toward us is and has always been good. But Adam's sin brought death to the whole world (Rom. 5:12). It relinquished man's authority into Satan's hands. Outside of covenant with God, Satan had the power to manipulate mankind, and he did so for thousands of years through sin and death. What we see in Job happened before Jesus stripped the devil of that authority. This is the oldest book in the Bible and occurred even before the Abrahamic Covenant. In the Old Testament, Satan had access to God's presence to argue his legal rights of dominion (Col. 2:15/ Job 1:6-12). Satan is actually coming into the presence of God and challenging God's blessing on Job's life. Why is God even discussing Job with Satan? God is not that hard up for fellowship! Satan is the one who brought Job up, not God. God simply acknowledged Satan's interest in Job, saying *"...Have you considered my servant Job?"* (Job 1:8). Satan had considered Job and wanted to challenge God's blessings on Job's life. He also brought into question Job's motives and reasons for serving God (Job 1:11). Satan has always been the accuser of the brethren (Rev. 12:10). The conversation between God and Satan in Job 1 reveals that Satan had been watching Job. Could it be that God was saying, "I know what you are doing Satan!" (Job 1:6-12). God's covenant with Abraham and Israel limited Satan's dominion. But Job didn't have a covenant with God. He lived outside God's legal protection. At that time, there was no mediator to stand in the gap for him. God even told the devil, *"Behold, all that he has is in your power; only do not lay a hand on his person"* (Job 1:12). Many view this statement as God giving Satan permission to assault Job rather than God simply acknowledging Satan's power over Job given by Adam in original sin. Satan is the god of this world (2 Cor. 4:4). Satan is the prince of the power of the air (Eph. 2:2-3).

God's covenant with Jesus changed all that. It destroyed Satan's dominion over the earth and gave us a mediator to stand before God (Heb. 12:24 / 1 Tim. 2:5). We are so blessed to be in covenant with God! The rights and protections we have under the new covenant far exceeds the old (Heb. 8:6). In this new covenant, Satan cannot do to us what he did to Job. Because of Jesus' death and resurrection, we have authority over his works (Matt. 28:18). But before God's covenants with His people, Satan had dominion over us through sin and Adam's transgression. We now have dominion over him through Jesus' victory and the gift of righteousness.

Many people misread the book of Job because they do not understand these things. They do not understand that Job sat outside covenant with God which allowed Satan to access his life. They do not understand that Job and Job's friends had no knowledge of Satan or his devices. These men attributed everything that happened in life to God, both the good and the bad. They viewed wealth as a reward for good behavior, and hardship as just punishment for bad behavior. They said things like:

> *...who ever perished being innocent? Or where were the upright ever cut off? Even as* **I have seen**, *those who plow iniquity and sow trouble reap the same. By the blast of God they perish, and by the breath of His anger they are consumed.*
>
> Job 4:7-9

All they knew was sowing and reaping, so in their minds it was whatever harvest is received was the one that was sown. They were limited by what they had seen. They were totally dominated by their senses and limited, carnal knowledge. They saw God at work in the tribulations of Job, saying:

> *Behold, happy is the man whom God corrects; Therefore do not despise the chastening of the Almighty. For He bruises, but He binds up; He wounds, but His hands make whole.*
>
> Job 5:17-18

Not much has changed. People still attribute evil to God. But God is not killing our kids. God is not afflicting our bodies or stealing our property, any more than He did Job's. That's Satan's role. Jesus said, *"The thief's purpose is to steal and kill and destroy. My purpose is to give them a rich and satisfying life"* (John 10:10, NLT). Job didn't do anything to cause his calamity. That was Satan's doing. And before you ask, no, God didn't "allow" it in the way people think. Just because God allows something doesn't mean He wills it. He allowed Adam to eat of the tree of the knowledge of good and evil but warned him of the consequences of his disobedience and told him not to eat (Gen. 2:17). He allowed Israel to have a king but did not will it (1 Sam. 8:7). He allowed Israel to put in evil rulers, but not by His hand. This is much like what we see happening in politics today: *"They have set up kings, **but not by me;** they have made princes, but I did not acknowledge them"* (Hosea 8:4 KJV). Not everyone in office today was placed there by God. God allows a lot of things He does not will. Never mistake what He allows as His will. God didn't send the devil to torment Job. God simply acknowledged what Satan had been doing—considering His servant, Job (Job 1:8; 2:3). Though Job did not understand this (and neither does much of the Church), he refused to lay the blame for his misfortunes on God, or confess under duress from his friends, a sin (seed sown) that brought about such a horrible consequence (harvest). Finally, at a point of despair, he cried out for God to reveal any hidden sin in his heart: "If I have caused this calamity, show me. Pardon me and take away my iniquity" (Job 7:20-21, paraphrased). I love this attitude. But Job's friends doubled down on him, condemned and pressured him to repent of some imagined sin. Over time Job grows weary. He knows he has not sinned to cause such destruction, but he begins to question God's justice.

In Job 6:30, Job asks, *"Is there iniquity in my tongue? Cannot my taste discern perverse things?"* (KJV). He is simply saying that if I had sown a seed this bad to reap such a horrific harvest, wouldn't I know it? His friends insisted he was lying and needed to come clean or even worse things would come upon him. Listen to Zophar's condemning speech: *"Listen! God is doubtless punishing you far less than you deserve!"* (Job 11:6 NLT). In other words, you deserve worse than what has happened to you. Worse things than losing ten kids, all your servants but one, and all your wealth in one day? Again, Job knew he hadn't sown to this harvest and defended his integrity; however, in his pain and weariness he questioned God's character and integrity towards the end of his trial (not good).

Eventually, Job's young friend, Elihu, speaks up. He rebukes Job for questioning God and rebukes the older friends for condemning Job without cause. He reminds them all of God's majesty and their relative position to that (Job 32-37). Then Elihu says, *"We cannot imagine the power of the Almighty; but even though he is just and righteous, he does not destroy us. No wonder people everywhere fear him. All who are wise show him reverence"* (Job 37:23-24, NLT). What a revelation from an Old Testament saint! Elihu was the only friend hearing God. He was the youngest as well, proving age doesn't necessarily make you wise, it just makes you old.

We are reminded of the patience of Job in the book of James. He refers to Job's end and the Lord's mercy (James 5:11). God's restitution to Job was so sweet that the latter days of his life were more blessed than his beginning, and Job received back twice as much as he ever lost (Job 42:10, 12). Let us remain faithful and patient knowing and understanding the goodness of God regardless of our circumstances. We need to be faithful to sow good seeds, but we must remain faithful even when our circumstances bring us something unexpected.

Dear ones, God has not changed. He is the same yesterday, today, and forever (Heb. 13:8). Though He is just and righteous, He does not destroy us, but rather is merciful. But sometimes we do reap where we did not sow. Like Job's friends, many in the body of Christ do not understand this truth. They condemn themselves or others, even blaming God, when they face hardship. They think, "How did this happen? This must be my fault." Or "Why is God doing this to me!?" The truth is not everything we reap is something to which we sowed to and God is only doing good to you. Jesus taught His disciples this in John chapter nine.

Jesus was leaving the temple when he passed a blind man. His disciples asked, *"Rabbi, who sinned, this man or his parents, that he was born blind?"* (John 9:2). The disciples were looking for a cause-and-effect relationship to explain this man's birth defect. We do this sometimes when we pray. We ask questions or seek answers based on our finite knowledge. We limit God's answer by our spiritual assumptions. We ask God is it A or B? But what if the answer is C? Notice how Jesus answered the disciples:

> *Neither this man nor his parents sinned, but that the works of God should be revealed in him. I must work the works of Him who sent Me while it is day; the night is coming when no one can work.*
>
> John 9:3-4

Neither the man nor his parents' personal sin caused this man to be born blind. But Jesus didn't say sin was not the cause of the blindness. Sin always leads to human suffering and death (Rom. 6:23). And while human suffering can be the wage of our personal sin, sometimes the death we experience is a result of Adam's sin and other people's rebellion to God (Rom. 5:12).

Years ago, a precious couple called me to pray for their young son. He had been diagnosed with cancer. Though they knew the healing power of God, they were not seeing the manifestation of healing in their son's body. As I talked with them, it became obvious that they were dealing with condemnation. They blamed themselves for their son's condition and were seeking God to find the sin that opened the door for Satan to afflict their son. That condemnation kept them from standing in faith to fight cancer. I shared this Kingdom mystery with them and encouraged them to "believe only." (It's hard to fight against something you think you caused.) Together, we submitted to God in prayer, rebuked and resisted the devil, and watched him flee. Their baby boy was healed! Hallelujah!

So, take heart. If you are experiencing difficult circumstances right now, don't assume you are to blame. We live in a fallen world. Bad things happen to good people all the time, just like Job. And while wisdom takes responsibility for what we have sown to, it also trusts God to justify or rescue us when we reap hardship where we did not sow. Seek God. If you need to repent, He will reveal that to you (Job 6:30). But keep sowing seeds of faith. Remember, we can sow to the future we desire.

In 1982, Sue and I were just getting started in ministry (and life). We were pastoring two Methodist churches in neighboring communities and ministering at an independent teaching center on Friday nights. Attendees were being blessed and wanted to share what they were learning with friends and family. They also wanted to be able to listen to the word over and over again so we started recording my messages.

At this point in our lives, we were barely getting by. We scraped together what we could to purchase a small cassette recorder. Then I found an inexpensive duplicator to reproduce the masters we were making. At first, we charged a small amount for the taped messages to try and cover our costs. But we understood the struggle of needing solid Biblical teaching and not being able to afford it, so we ran as many sales as possible. We did half-price sales, birthday sales, anniversary sales, you-got-up-this-morning sales, and whatever else we could think of to allow as many people as possible to have access to the messages.

One night while wrestling over the tape ministry, I felt God gently and sweetly drop a word into my heart. *"Freely you have received, freely give"* (Matt. 10:8).

Freely give? How? We couldn't afford to purchase all those tapes! We weren't making ends meet as it was. (At the time I didn't know anyone else who was giving their stuff away, so I argued with God over that word all night. Not smart! Wrestling with God accomplished nothing but sleep deprivation.) I reasoned that if I obeyed and gave away our tapes for free, we wouldn't lose anything. People probably wouldn't take them anyway. But what if they did? Could we give the messages away and still be good stewards? Would we plunge the ministry into inescapable debt?

Again, I heard the Lord whisper to my spirit, *"Freely you have received, freely give."* Suddenly, the revelation of seedtime and harvest flooded my heart and faith rose up within me. I knew if I would sow God's Word, He would give back to me *"pressed down, shaken together, and running over"* (Luke 6:38). I knew the revelation of grace and truth as a seed and when sowed I would reap a harvest. My greatest desire then and still today is to get truth to God's people so they can know it and experience freedom (John 8:31-32). I knew God would download revelation to me as I studied, and our needs would be met. I simply needed to obey. Much of the revelation I had was reaped from others and I was entering into their labors. I needed to now sow to my future.

"Yes Lord," I said aloud. "I will give them away." Immediately, great peace flooded my heart. Then Sue woke up. "What did you agree to?" she asked. I told her, in fear and trembling. But Sue didn't struggle to believe and obey as I had. She was glad I had finally settled the matter in my heart and went back to sleep, only believing.

Today, I can truthfully say that we have never looked back on that decision with any kind of regret. There were times we didn't know if we would make it, but God was faithful. And He continues to be. We sowed to the future we desired, and to date, we have given away over 100 million messages—for free!

Dear ones, none of us have to be victims of circumstance. God has made us all victors in Christ. In Romans 8:35 Paul asks the question— *"Who shall separate us from the love of Christ? Shall tribulation, or distress, or persecution, or famine, or nakedness, or peril, or sword?"* Then Paul answers that question in verse 37—*"Nay, in all these things we are **more** than conquerors through him that loved us"* (KJV). Paul goes on to declare that he was confident that nothing could separate us from God's love in Christ Jesus (Rom. 8:38-39).

Sowing and reaping plays a big part in our ability to experience a more than a conqueror's life. But never fall into the trap of thinking that because you have sowed, God now "owes" you a specific harvest. God's provision and blessings are ours by grace. Faith is our seed sown, reaping a harvest of grace. Because Jesus came and destroyed the works of the devil, we have access to this inheritance:

> *"I will rebuke the devourer for your sakes, so that he will not destroy the **fruit of your ground**, nor shall the vine fail to bear fruit for you in the field," says the LORD of hosts.*
>
> Malachi 3:11

That was an old covenant promise under an inferior covenant. We have a better covenant established on better promises (Heb. 8:6). In the name of Jesus in partnership with Him we can rebuke Satan and he will flee, and he cannot destroy the fruit of our ground, but our fruit shall remain. No wonder Peter declares this salvation to be *"joy unspeakable and full of glory"* (1 Peter 1:8 KJV).

Let's be thankful. Let's keep mixing faith with God's goodness and participating in the immutable laws of His Kingdom. And let's remember that not only are we reaping what we sow, we are also the benefactors of reaping where we did not sow.

> *Do you not say, 'There are still four months and then comes the harvest?' Behold, I say to you, lift up your eyes and look at the fields, for they are already white for harvest! And he who reaps receives wages, and gathers fruit for eternal life, that both he who sows and he who reaps may rejoice together. For in this the saying is true: 'One sows and another reaps.' I sent you to **reap that for which you have not labored**; others have labored, and you have entered into their labors.*
>
> John 4:35-38

God revealed this mystery and principle with Israel when they entered their promised land. They didn't receive a desolate land, but rather they reaped a land with houses, wells, vineyards, and gardens—all things they did not labor to produce (Deut. 6:11). They reaped where they did not sow. They enjoyed the harvest of other's labors. This is a picture of God's grace in our lives. In grace we reap where we did not sow.

Wow! We are reaping a great harvest off seeds we did not sow. First, we are reaping off the life Jesus sowed as a seed. We did nothing to deserve the grace of God. Yet each day we respond to His grace by faith, we reap His Kingdom. We reap the rewards of His Name. We reap His Spirit, the armor of God, peace, joy, righteousness, and free access to the Throne of Grace. We are so blessed.

We are also reaping a harvest of seeds planted by the saints who have gone before us—the apostles, the early church leaders at Nicaea, Martin Luther (who saw the corruption sneaking into the church and spurred the Protestant Reformation), and William Tyndale (who gave his life to ensure we had a copy of the scriptures in English). We reap a harvest from the founders of this nation who sought God's wisdom as they crafted a new form of government to ensure we could worship God without fear of persecution, prosecution, or execution for our faith. They fashioned a Bill of Rights that protects us from the government. These are rights that come from God that limit what government can do. WOW! What a blessing. Unfortunately, many have not recognized this blessing. And instead of sowing seeds to ensure that harvest continues, they have neglected that field. Now weeds are growing in it, and we are slowly losing our harvest on freedom.

We certainly need to be mindful of the seeds we sow, brothers and sisters. We will reap a harvest off them. But we need to keep this truth in balance with the truth that we reap where we did not sow, for both good and bad: *"A false balance is an abomination to the Lord, but a just weight is his delight"* (Prov. 11:1 ESV). God delights when we choose to walk discerning the balance of His Word. Don't be quick to judge a harvest, yours or others around you.

But seek God for wisdom. Praise Him for every good seed and subsequent harvest and resist the temptation to be discouraged when you face the bad. Be steadfast in your faith and know that He can work it all for good to all of us who love Him and are called according to His purpose (Rom. 8:28-29).

Salvation Prayer

If your heart desires connection with your Heavenly Father and to live in the blessing of His family, there is hope in Christ Jesus. If you have not made Jesus Lord of your life but would like to do so, you can simply pray this:

> *"Father, I come to you today; I confess I'm not right, but I want to be right and make things right. I cannot do enough or quit enough to save myself, I need help. I believe Jesus is that help. I believe He came to this earth, lived a perfect life, and died on the cross for me. He bore my sins and the punishment for all my sins. He died, was buried, and rose again on the third day. I now confess Him as Lord, King, and Savior. Thank you for forgiving me and cleansing me of all my sin and changing me in my heart. Help me now to serve you all the days of my life, with all my heart. Amen!"*

If you prayed this prayer and received Jesus in your heart today, let us know and we will send you a free book! Contact us at 580-634-5665 or dsm@pastorduane.com

GRACE & TRUTH

Join Duane as he boldly teaches Biblical wisdom mixed with his unique sense of humor, offering hope & revelation for today's world.

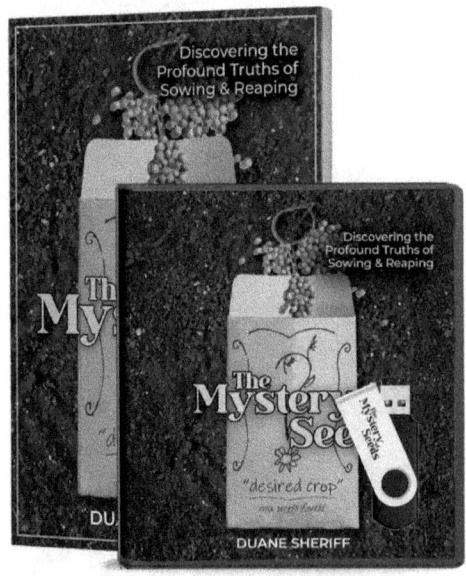

USB Bundle "The Mystery Of Seeds" is perfect for small groups, home churches, bible studies, and your personal relationship with the Lord.

Includes: printed booklet, Grace & Truth broadcast series (audio and video files), a printable workbook, and study notes for each episode.

About The Author

Duane Sheriff has been in ministry for over four decades. He is an author, international apostolic teacher, conference speaker and founder of Victory Life Church. He is known for his humor and ability to present the Gospel with clarity and simplicity. He is passionate about helping people discover their identity and grow in Christ through his unique biblical insights.

His first book, *Identity Theft*, was released in 2017. Since then, he has authored several more books including *Divine Guidance, Rhythms of Grace, Erasing Offense, Counterculture,* and *Children As Arrows*. He also serves as an adjunct instructor at Charis Bible School, and hosts "Grace & Truth," a daily television broadcast. Duane and his wife, Sue, were married in 1980 and have four children, who have blessed them with numerous grandchildren. For additional study resources or free teachings visit our website at **www.pastorduane.com**

CONTACT INFORMATION

Duane Sheriff Ministries

PO Box 427, Durant, OK

dsm@pastorduane.com

Helpline (Mon. – Fri. 8am-5pm CT)

580-404-0376

www.pastorduane.com

www.ingramcontent.com/pod-product-compliance
Lightning Source LLC
Chambersburg PA
CBHW062117080426
42734CB00012B/2894